CONGREGATIONAL LEADERSHIP
IN ANXIOUS TIMES

Congregational Leadership in Anxious Times

Being Calm and Courageous No Matter What

Peter L. Steinke

THE
ALBAN
INSTITUTE

Herndon, Virginia
www.alban.org

The Alban Institute
2121 Cooperative Way, Suite 100
Herndon, VA 20171

Scripture quotations, unless otherwise noted, are from the New Revised
Standard Version of the Bible, © 1989, Division of Christian Education
of the National Council of Churches of Christ in the United States of
America, and are used by permission.

Scripture quotations marked RSV are from the Revised Standard Version
of the Bible, copyright © 1952 [2nd edition, 1971] by the Division of
Christian Education of the National Council of the Churches of Christ in
the United States of America. Used by permission. All rights reserved.

Cover design by Concept Foundry.

Library of Congress Cataloging-in-Publication Data

Steinke, Peter L.
  Congregational leadership in anxious times : being calm and courageous
no matter what / Peter L. Steinke.
      p. cm.
  Includes bibliographical references.
  ISBN-13: 978-1-56699-328-9
  ISBN-10: 1-56699-328-8
  1. Christian leadership. I. Title.

BV652.1.S725 2006
252--dc22
                                        2006036119

    10   09   08   07   06   VG   1   2   3   4   5

Contents

Foreword

Practical wisdom. That's what Peter Steinke offers readers in *Congregational Leadership in Anxious Times.* Throughout this long-awaited book, Steinke is faithful to Scripture, conveys deep insight into the human condition, provides a clear exposition of systems thinking and Bowen theory, and offers us a look at some of the fascinating situations he has seen in his 20 years of consultation with congregations and church leaders.

Peter Steinke is a gift. Equipped as a pastor and counselor, he emerged soon after he began serving parishes as an effective consultant to congregations in crisis. He continues to fill that role, yet perhaps his greatest gift is his capacity to foster health, rather than simply to pick up the pieces after a crisis. I have known Pete for nearly 20 years, served on an advisory board for his Healthy Congregations materials, and have been privileged to see him work in a host of settings. His insights into life, especially the complex relationships of Christian community, are prolific and profound. Even better, he models in his daily life what he teaches in his books and consultations.

Life—particularly life in Christian community—is rife with differences, and conflict is seldom far from us. Although conflicting views, stances, and opinions are a given, however, chaos and crisis need not follow. Whether conflicting approaches to mission and ministry lead to creativity and growth or to polarized stand-offs is largely a matter of how the key leaders are able to respond to the situation. While we may be tempted to lament or hide when conflicts swirl into our lives, Peter Steinke provides practical insight and wise counsel for more productive ways to respond in the midst of the difficulties.

Whether you are already familiar with Bowen theory of systems thinking or not, the scenarios will ring true and the counsel will make sense. When I read this book, I recognized myself, my colleagues, and the congregations I have served, and I think you will have the same experience.

I have seen "anxious times" manifest themselves in many ways, and no doubt you have too. Is your church council polarizing over a minor issue? Do you have to confront the custodian? Does the activity in the narthex seem more hostile than hospitable? Do you dread the monthly treasurer's report? Have the "well-meaning" questions about your ministry begun to raise nagging doubts? Do expectations of you seem to outpace your time and energy? Has the congregation been stressed by community strife? These and other "anxious times" are all too familiar to most of us.

Not only do I recognize the situations Steinke describes; I recognize myself in them. I admit that throughout my 37 years of ordained ministry, there have been times when I have not been as calm and courageous as I might have been, and it would have been easy for Steinke to write about calm and courageous leadership in such a way that I might feel judged or scolded. Fortunately, however, the practical wisdom in this book is also gracious. I don't come away feeling ashamed or inadequate; rather, I hear acknowledgment that in anxious times "all of us fall short," and I find insightful counsel on how to navigate similar situations better in the future.

There have also been times when I have indeed been calm and courageous. I thank God for those times. What I need, though, is some sense of how to behave the same way in the future. What I hope for is a little like hitting a really good golf shot. It's wonderful to hit one, but the real question is whether I can learn to repeat it regularly. So it is with calm, courageous leadership. We all manage it now and then. This book can help us repeat it more regularly.

If your congregation is experiencing smooth sailing right now, this will be good preventative medicine. If you are feeling some of the cold winds of controversy, it will help you navigate them and stay healthy. If you are afraid you are about to capsize, this may help you right the ship. In any case, you will find the practical wisdom in this book to be a gift.

Bishop Rick Foss
Eastern North Dakota Synod (ELCA)

Preface

In *Congregational Leadership in Anxious Times: Being Calm and Courageous No Matter What,* I share with church leaders many of the insights and experiences I have discovered working with congregations nationwide. From numerous wise people, a multitude of difficult situations, and a solid sampling of positive happenings, I have learned that no group shapes and influences a congregation's health, efficiency, and growth more than church leaders. The way in which the leader functions arises out of who the leader is. The leader's *being* and *functioning* are twin to each other.

My hope is that the ideas, stories, realities, and provocations in this book will both *enlighten* and *embolden* your leadership in the local congregation. Knowing and understanding what is happening is certainly significant. But awareness is not enough. Someone has to be bold enough to suggest or take action.

My experience encompasses work with more than 150 congregations of different sizes (about 100 to 4,000 members), in places ranging from New Hampshire to California and Florida to Washington, with histories dating from the 18th century to a freshly minted congregation, and from eight denominational affiliations.

Influencing my thinking significantly is Bowen Theory,[1] an understanding of what happens when people come together and interact, how they mutually influence each other's behaviors, how change in one person affects another, and how they create something larger than themselves. The genius of the theory is that it makes visible what is invisible. It presents concepts that give insight into human behavior. At the core of the theory are two *variables—the degree of anxiety* and *the capacity to differentiate.* With anxiety intensifying and penetrating more areas of our lives, even in the church, *leaders today cannot be as anxious as the people they serve.* To lead means to have some command of our own anxiety and some capacity not to let other people's anxiety contaminate us; that is, not to allow their anxiety to affect our thinking, actions, and decisions.

Central to my thinking is also my understanding of the biblical idea of the *imago dei.* When we ask what is the intended or essential character and vocation of the creature, Christian theology turns to the symbol of the *imago dei.* As reflections of the divine form of life, humans are responsive, relational creatures. To be created in the likeness of God means God created someone who corresponds to him—to whom God can speak and give, to whom God can invite and bless. The creature is created for relationship and specifically the relationship designated by the biblical word *love.* In loving God and one another we image God. "God is love, and those who abide in love abide in God, and God abides in them" (1 John 4:16b).

The creature's vocation, given and enabled by God, is to relate to God as a partner in covenant—"They shall be my people, and I will be their God" (Jer. 32:38)—and to join in compassion with the human family to reflect the love of God. "If I speak in the tongues of mortals and of angels . . . And if I have prophetic powers, and understand all mysteries and all knowledge . . . but do not have love, I am nothing" (1 Cor. 13:1, 2).

In this book I supply no automatic answers or plump solutions to the challenges of anxious times. But you will discover examples, insights, illustrations, and hints for your leadership role. I am grateful for the many capable, faithful, and committed lay leaders and pastors I have met. I hope theirs as well as my own insights carry you through rough times, provide clarity during confusing times, and uplift you in joyous times. Even more, I intend to encourage you, because I know you will need courage to maintain the course, to unearth the secrets, to resist the sabotaging of your efforts, to withstand the group's fury, and to overcome your own timidity or doubts. The courage will be well spent because anxious times hold not only the potential for destruction but also for creation, important learnings, and changes that will strengthen the congregation.

I have intended this material to be a resource for judicatory personnel, for pastors, for professional church workers, and especially for lay leaders. The book is divided into three parts: "The Leader's Presence," "The Leader's Functioning," and "The Leader's Challenges." Each part has three chapters. "The Leader's Presence" contains reflections on Bowen Theory and its relationship to leadership. You may encounter new words, phrases, and ideas, but a careful reading of this section will certainly enlighten the other two sections of the book. Because it has information for special circumstances in anxious times, I have included in "Postscript," at the end of the book, an article I had previously written. The vignettes and stories about congregations come from my experiences, but they are modified to avoid identification. You will notice that the leader's being and functioning were critical to good outcomes in each of the situations. As I have noted in my book *Healthy Congregations: A Systems Approach,* leaders are essential to the ultimate well-being of the congregation:

> Like healthy people, systems promote their health through "responsible and enlightened behavior." The people who are most in position to enhance the health of a system are precisely those who have been empowered to be responsible, namely the leaders. They are the chief stewards, they are the people who are willing to be accountable for the welfare of the system. They set a tone, invite collaboration, make decisions, map a direction, establish boundaries, encourage self-expression, restrain what threatens the integrity of the whole, and keep the system's direction aligned with purposes.[2]

Acknowledgments

Many people have contributed to this volume. There are the unnamed congregational leaders and members who have influenced my thinking through their wisdom, counsel, and especially courageous action. They deeply cared for their congregations in such a way that they were willing to risk the displeasure of others, even to the point of being demonized. In some cases, they refused to exchange what they considered to be the truth for a return to placid conditions. They resisted giving in to the pressure of the moment if it meant forsaking their integrity. Some leaders patiently and calmly stayed connected to people with opposing viewpoints and to those known to be troublesome. Nonetheless, these leaders never shied away from challenging their congregations and never hesitated to ask probing questions. To their credit, they did not regard their own judgments as placing them on higher moral ground. They simply could not set aside distressing circumstances or avoid a difficult decision even if it meant individuals would be hurt or the congregation would suffer. They spoke "the truth in love" (Eph. 4:15) so that the truth could set people free (John 8:32).

My appreciation also extends to a group of leaders that I want to name, those who carefully read the first draft of this book, making significant suggestions for improvements in content, style, and structure. They represent different denominations and a variety of positions in the church:

Ben Becksvoort (Christian Reformed, Executive for Missions)
Bev Becksvoort (Christian Reformed, Educator)

Steven Johns-Boehme (Disciples of Christ, Associate Regional
   Minister)
Jim Boyer (Lutheran, Pastoral Counselor)
Rick Foss (Lutheran, Bishop)
Larry Foster (Lutheran, Educator/Trainer)
Craig Gilliam (Methodist, Church Consultant)
Ron Rehrer (Lutheran, Pastoral Counselor)
Deborah Rundlett (Presbyterian, Church Executive)
Bill Snyder (Lutheran, Parish Pastor)
Gerry Tyer (Presbyterian, Church Executive)
David Verner (Presbyterian, Pastoral Counselor)
Sallie Verner (Presbyterian, Educator)

My wife, Kelly, and my son Tim helped me greatly during my period of recovery after surgery. During this period, I wrote the book. Their patience and assistance was indispensable.

PART 1

THE LEADER'S PRESENCE

People vary considerably in how they address emotionally challenging events. On the lower (immature) side, people are *reactive*. They blame more often; they criticize harshly; they take offense easily; they focus on others; they want instant solutions; they cannot see the part they play in problems. On the higher (mature) side, people are more thoughtful and reflective; they act on principle, not instinct; they can stand back and observe. They are *responsive*. Intent and choice characterize their behavior.

The leader's capacity to be in conscious control over (to respond to) automatic functioning (reaction) affects the well-being of the whole community. The leader's "presence" can have a calming influence on reactive behavior. Rather than reacting to the reactivity of others, leaders with self-composure and self-awareness both exhibit and elicit a more thoughtful response. In part 1, you will discover how your handling of self is a major factor in anxious times.

Chapter 1

Anxious Souls

In this chapter we will explore the levels of anxiety—the first of two key concepts of Bowen Theory—and examine anxiety's effect on a congregation and your role as a congregational leader.

Anxiety is an automatic reaction "to a threat, real or imagined."[1] As a startle reaction, anxiety protects you from potential risk or harm. Anxiety is a natural reaction designed for self-preservation. Our Creator has provided us with a strong urge for survival. At one level, anxiety can make us alert, more self-conscious, and highly motivated to take action. At an elevated level, however, anxiety can be a paralyzer (the word anxiety is derived from a word meaning "to choke" or "to cause pain by squeezing"). If intense and prolonged, anxiety has a strangling effect, depleting people's energy, disturbing their thinking, and dividing their loyalties.

Being naturally anxious souls, we find anxious times to be a real challenge to leadership. At the beginning of this study, we will see how anxiety at elevated levels shapes and influences people's thinking and behavior.

3

In Anxious Times

As a congregational leader, you come to your position with enthusiasm and hope. Your commitment is genuine. You anticipate making a difference in your congregation's life through your service. Much of your service as a congregational leader will be satisfying and enjoyable. You will be involved with routine oversight—ratifying changes in budget or staff, clarifying policies or procedures, perhaps occasionally settling a minor dispute, offering new challenges, and supporting staff and congregation. Joining with other committed believers will be a blessing as you observe their care for others, their appreciation for the congregation's efforts, and their guidance in setting a direction for the future. In turn, you may be a blessing to them, supporting them in a time of need or sharing responsibility with them for an area of ministry.

With a gradual or sudden elevation of anxiety in your congregation, a different tone or mood develops. You sense a shift of spirit; you hear rumblings. A special meeting of the church leaders is arranged. The minute you arrive at church, you know something is different. The usual lighthearted banter and general chatter has given way to serious silence. You are informed of the startling news. Your leadership role will take on a different dimension now.

Suddenly or gradually you are tested. Any number of unexplained circumstances may arise:

- The church building burns and is a charred tomb.
- The pastor is accused of sexual misconduct or harrassment, leaving members with anger, embarrassment, and a sense of betrayal.

5

- When the organist/choir director is asked to resign under a cloak of silence, financial offerings decline to protest the decision or to leverage a reversal of the decision.
- Brutal e-mails are exchanged between two lay leaders who favor different theological positions, and they are widely disseminated and fracture the community.
- The pastor commits suicide, and a wrenching period of grief and guilt ensues.
- Three youth from the congregation die in an alcohol-related automobile accident, leaving people psychically numb.
- Two staff members distribute a petition requesting an unambiguous policy on what marriage is and who can be married.
- A beloved founding minister disappears, leaving no clue as to his whereabouts, only to be found living with a new partner of the same sex and avoiding any contact with his wife and children.
- Job outsourcing leaves a small town with scant employment opportunities, ushering in harsh economic days for families in the church.
- A small band of influential members oppose the pastor, citing isolated events or little proof to buttress their steady stream of criticism.
- A natural disaster partially destroys the church building and disrupts the lives of more than half of the congregation.

These tensions and traumas leave their mark on congregational life. Likewise, transitional times present a similar set of anxieties. Such transitions might include:

- The relocation of the church building
- The initiation of a new ministry to serve immigrants moving into the area, most of whom don't know English
- Promotion of a fresh emphasis on justice and peace concerns

- Reexamination of the congregation's mission
- A steady loss of major leaders
- Developing new ties with other congregations and learning to share resources
- Movement to a more conservative or liberal approach in doctrine and practices
- The known but unspoken recognition that the congregation is aging and not attracting new families is finally named
- The replacement of a senior pastor who had the skill to manage the great diversity in the congregation
- A splintered congregation trying to find ways to pump up energy and to heal deep hurts

Nothing new under the sun—especially nothing controversial—happens without confusion, resistance, or emotional reactivity. All of the previously cited tensions, traumas, and transitions leave a trail of anxiety. This is where you enter the story. Anxiety alone will not harm or endanger a system. How anxiety is addressed will determine outcome more than anything. Your responsible and enlightened behavior will influence the situation more than any other action.

The Effects of Anxiety

The effects of anxiety on human thinking and behavior can be either positive or negative. Anxiety's negative effects on people's behavior can be the beginning of trouble and dissension. We will look closely at three of these effects—the repressive, the infectious, and the reactive.

The Repressive Effects

Anxiety comes from an interesting family of words. The great-grandfather is the Greek *ananke,* meaning "throat" or "to press together." In fact, *Ananke* was the name of the Greek god of constraint who presided over slavery. *Ananke* was the word used for the yokes or rings on the necks of slaves. Anxiety can hold us back, take us by the throat, and chain us like a slave. Consider some of *ananke's* relatives:

angr (Indo-European)	anger
angst (German)	general dread
angra (Old Norse)	grief
angustus (Latin)	anguish
eng (German)	narrow
angere (Latin)	to choke or strangle
angina (English)	the tight sensation in the chest that accompanies dread

This family of words expresses tightness, narrowness, and suffocation. The same sense of anxiety as constraint is reflected in the Old Testament. The psalmist frequently uses the word *zarar,* "human distress." "In my distress I called upon the LORD; to my God I cried for help" (Ps. 18:6). *Zarar* is literally translated "narrow space." Anxiety tightens: we think in a narrow-minded way or behave in predictable patterns. The antonym of *zarar* is *yasha,* signifying "open space." In fact, *yasha* can also be translated "salvation" (the base word for *Yeshua* or Jesus). "The LORD is my light and my salvation; whom shall I fear?" (Ps. 27:1). Being less anxious, we feel relaxed because there's room to breathe. People feel expansive and joyful when they have open space or freedom.

Anxiety affects human functioning by tightening thinking or restraining behavior. Look at what anxiety does to repress a person:

- decreases our capacity to learn
- replaces curiosity with a demand for certainty
- stiffens our position over against another's
- interrupts concentration

- floods the nervous system, so that we cannot hear what is said without distortion or cannot respond with clarity
- simplifies ways of thinking (yes/no; either/or)
- prompts a desire for a quick fix
- arouses feelings of helplessness or self-doubt
- leads to an array of defensive behaviors
- diminishes flexibility in response to life's challenges
- creates imaginative gridlock (not being able to think of alternatives, options, or new perspectives)

Note some of the repressive effects of anxiety in the following vignette.

Raymond Marshall, a longtime member of Broadway Church, and Sheila Walker, a newer member, demonstrably oppose the recommended building programs. Raymond contends that the estimate of what the congregation could raise in pledges ($1.8 million) is bloated. His own appraisal is $1.2 million. If the proposal passes, Raymond announces he will not contribute to it. To derail the project, Raymond sends out an e-mail to more than 70 members detailing reasons to deny the leadership's request for building a new family life center. Meanwhile Sheila Walker tells the younger families at Broadway about "the horror story of her sister's congregation." After a building program of similar size, that congregation lost membership even though the inducement to build was based on growth.

When the leadership asks to speak with Raymond and Sheila, both refuse, saying the leaders won't listen and the meeting would only be a facade. They continue their opposition, in spite of the leadership's deal that if they can raise $1.8 million in pledges in the next couple of months, the two of them would cease their resistance. Utterly convinced of his own estimate, Raymond Marshall refuses to cooperate. Sheila Walker says people will pledge more than they can give in order to build the new center. Sensing that the project is in jeopardy, the leaders decide to delay the vote on the proposal to plot a counter move.

Sheila and Raymond demonstrate the following repressive effects of anxiety: Raymond Marshall demands certainty, stiffens his position against others, and simplifies everything into "this" or "that." He's not motivated to hear. Sheila reacts because of her sister's experience. And she thinks narrowly when she assumes that people will pledge more than they will give in order to approve the building project.

The Infectious Effects

Anxiety is also contagious. It connects people. Let one or two people unleash their anxiety, and it won't be long before it has a ripple effect on the congregation. Bowen distinguished acute anxiety from chronic anxiety. Acute anxiety is situational and time-based. It is a momentary loss of self-composure and poise. As the reactivity scales down, the "fever" quickly runs its course. People are back on track again. Chronic anxiety is a more powerful infectant. Chronic anxiety is perpetually present in someone or structured into a relationship. Simply stated, chronic anxiety is not specific to a threat. Any issue, topic, or circumstance can provoke chronically anxious people. Consequently, they have little capacity to step out of their experience, observe their own emotionality, reflect on what is happening, make choices based in principles, and manage their lives.

An example of acute anxiety in the Bible is seen in the disciple Peter. While warming his hands over a fire, Peter is recognized by Roman soldiers. Believing they saw Peter in the Garden of Gethsemane, they ask him if he was with Jesus. Peter denies knowing the man called Jesus, three times. With the crowing of the cock, Peter remembers the words of Jesus. Luke tells us he left the fireplace, went outside, and "wept bitterly" (22:62). Chronic anxiety seemed to accompany the Israelites wandering in the wilderness. It all started when the people of God, nostalgic for their Egyptian diet spiced by garlic and sweetened by melon, became hungry. God sent manna. At first they gathered it up excitedly and were content and grateful. Soon they were displeased once again. As people do when times get hard, they expressed their bitterness. "We detest this miserable food" (Num. 21:5). Not only did they murmur against the Lord (Exod. 16:7), they also raised an outcry against their leader Moses. "Why did you bring us out of Egypt, to kill us and our children and livestock with thirst?" (Exod. 17:3). Before long, the people's impatience erupted into the demand for the visible presence of God. With Moses absent on Mount Sinai, his older brother, Aaron, succumbs to the people's petulant anxiety. They build a golden calf.

Two New Testament writers, Luke and John, use the Greek verb *goggizo* (to grumble, murmur, complain, or speak secretly) on several occasions:

> And the Pharisees and the scribes murmured, saying, "This man receives sinners and eats with them" (Luke 15:2, RSV).
> Now during those days, when the disciples were increasing in number, the Hellenists complained against the Hebrews because their widows were being neglected in the daily distribution of food (Acts 6:1).
> The Pharisees and their scribes were complaining to his disciples, saying, "Why do you eat and drink with tax collectors and sinners?" (Luke 5:30).
> Then the Jews began to complain about him because he said, "I am the bread that came down from heaven" (John 6:41).
> But Jesus, being aware that his disciples were complaining about it, said to them, "Does this offend you?" (John 6:61).

The Israelites, the Pharisees, the Hellenists, the Jews, and the disciples prefigure the complainers in the contemporary church. Grumbling is apparently endemic to human beings and, among some, epidemic. Put people together and their anxiety inevitably spreads like an infectious disease.

[handwritten margin note: Bible ↓ contagious grumbling]

The Reactive Effect

Many observers believe that the news media uses anxiety to arouse and arrest our attention. It exaggerates small dangers into national nightmares. It "plays on our fears," as we say. For instance, a shark attacks a swimmer. It's reported in the newspaper and on television's evening news. Anxiety about identical attacks intensifies, even though, as neuroscientist Richard Restak notes, the odds are 94,900,000 to 1 that a shark will attack you. The odds for drowning are much worse, 225,000 to 1.[2] No one, however, warns you against swimming.

Twenty-four-hour news programs feature commentators and guests who can put an edge to an issue and arouse the viewer's anxiety. The goal obviously is to stir up reactivity in people to keep them riveted to their channel. Disseminating information may not be the only goal of the "news." The newscasters want our reactivity, so we stayed tuned.

Reactivity is automatic. No thought goes into our action. An instinctive imperative drives our behavior. This, unfortunately, happens too routinely in congregations, particularly when a major upheaval occurs. All of the regressive effects noted beforehand come into play. Strange as it seems, some anxious congregations refuse to *see* their problems. People have a strong tendency to deny troubles—as if the difficulties should not be present, as if "Don't disturb" signs are hung on every door. Not recognizing a problem is an anxious defense. As pressure mounts, people's blindness may give way to begrudging acknowledgment. Even then, the congregation's reticence to act may be equal to their resistance to see. Still, anxiety denied has a habit of staying around and festering.

Closely related to denial is oversimplification. Congregations *simplify* by using comments like, "That just happens" or "Things were worse before." To neutralize or minimize their difficulties, congregations may react by portraying conditions as minor. Leaders sandpaper rough edges with glib remarks. They varnish the situation like wood to give a shiny picture of things. This behavior has a long history. The prophet Jeremiah lamented, "They have treated the wound of my people carelessly, saying, 'Peace, peace,' when there is no peace" (Jer. 6:14).

In other cases, individual lay leaders may apply themselves to specific challenges, but they receive little or no support from others. Discouraged, they may surrender to the disinterest, slowly drifting away from active participation, perhaps exiting from membership. *Ignoring* can be reactive. And the opportunity for learning and change disappears with the ignored leaders' inactivity or departure.

When facing anxious times, a high percentage of congregations *freeze.* Since action might trigger opposition, leaders delay and delay. No one wants to upset or offend others. Immobility can put off the inevitable, but only momentarily. As long as the congregation is stuck, it remains knee-deep in anxiety. Edwin Friedman, author of *Generation to Generation* and a student of Murray Bowen, has claimed: "Actually religious institutions are the worst offenders of encouraging immaturity and irresponsibility. In church after church some member is passive-aggressively holding the whole system hostage, and no one wants to fire him or force her to leave because it wouldn't be 'the Christian thing to do.' It has nothing to do with Christianity. Synagogues also tolerate abusers because it wouldn't be 'the Christian thing to do.'"[3] Indecisiveness is reactivity. It's a defense against a split in the house.

When anxiety ushers in its relatives—anger, anguish, and grief—the temptation to *scapegoat* is strong. Scapegoating is an attempt to pinpoint a culprit or to find fault with someone. The blame throwers at first will hurl charges indiscriminately at any target. Most likely, however, anxiety will be projected onto people in the most responsible or the most vulnerable positions in the congregation.

Blindness, simplification, disinterest, paralysis, and projection—all betray a congregation's inability to handle anxiety. It's as if the motto is, "Don't trouble us." If these anxious reactivities dominate a congregation, leaders will not be well equipped to use adversity for opportunity.

A Personal Note

I hope to assist you in avoiding such reactions. I want to encourage you to counter your own impulses to defend against trouble or distressing news with thoughtful reflection leading to responsible action. As a leader, you will be called upon to confront immature behavior. You will be surprised by the unexpected. You will be thrown into a position of naming a wrong or some ghost. Perhaps the most bizarre reactions you will encounter will be the resistance of people to you when you are functioning well. Immature citizens of the community may sabotage your efforts, since at some level they know they are losing control. You will be expected to soothe and comfort the distraught. You will be expected to sound the trumpet to avoid the school of anxiety. Yet, as novelist John Updike remarked, some things are hidden in health but revealed in 104-degree fever.[4] Certainly Paul understood this. Writing to the Romans, he said, "We ... boast in our sufferings, knowing that suffering produces endurance, and endurance produces character, and character produces hope, and hope does not disappoint us" (Rom. 5:3–5).

Working with anxious congregations, I always remind them that they have invited me to help them not to waste their suffering. The leader will need to challenge the congregation, anxious souls as they may be, to use anxious times as a springboard for change, learning, and different functioning. What is at stake may be the very vocation to which God has called and gathered these people together—their ministry and mission.

The Leader's Notebook

Thirteen Triggers of Anxiety for Congregations

What are the most common triggers of anxiety in congregations? The thirteen noted below are not listed in any particular order. One alone, if emotionally driven, could create havoc. Usually five or six happen serially or simultaneously, setting off anxious reactivity. Glance at the list and mentally note which ones your congregation has experienced in the last few years, or check which ones might ignite the most fury in your congregation. If you are going through a period of intense anxiety, remember anxiety is normal. It would happen in other congregations besides your own. The critical factor in determining outcome is the leadership's response to crisis.

1. Money: Follow the money trail—how to raise it, how to distribute it, how to manage when there isn't enough.

2. Sex, Sexuality: As sources of identity and self-expression, questions and differences pertaining to sex set off survival reactions.

3. Pastor's Leadership Style: Sometimes this is a euphemism for not liking the pastor. Sometimes it's a genuine concern that the needed leadership is not happening. Sometimes clergy and other leaders fail to determine what kind of leadership is needed.

4. Lay Leadership Style: Lay leaders can run the spectrum from hands-off to hands-on, from enabling to threatening, from expressing a failure of

nerve to demonstrating strength of conviction and courage.

5. Growth, Survival: Congregations may be anxious because growth is slow or worship attendance declines.

6. Boundaries: Boundary problems could include how much of a congregation's resources are given away and how much retained locally; people overstepping their authority; misuse of finances.

7. Trauma, Transition: A key or nodal event happens with a significant emotional impact, such as storm damage to the church structure or the retirement of a pastor after a long tenure.

8. Staff Conflict, Resignation: When the church staff is at odds or a staff member departs under a cloud of suspicion or for unexpected reasons, people become upset.

9. Harm Done to a Child, Death of a Child: Congregations are children sensitive. If a child is hurt or if one dies, there is a sense of helplessness: we cannot even protect or defend those in our care.

10. Old and New: Tension brews when considering a new hymnal to replace an old hymnal, to change the old time of worship, or to modify the receiving of a sacrament.

11. Contemporary and Traditional Worship: This is a special case of old and new. Immense emotionality is connected to styles of worship. The first murder in

really??? ←   sacred history, the story of Cain and Abel, involved
worship.

12. Gap between the Ideal and the Real: When high and
lofty ideas are betrayed by reality or when a focus on
mission degenerates into a focus on self-concerns,
people become disturbed.

13. Building, Construction, Space, and Territory: Add
or tear down a building; modify existing space;
move offices into new area; sell land or parsonage;
relocate. Anxiety will rise.

duh!!   In their study of why clergy leave local church ministry, Dean
R. Hoge and Jacqueline E. Wenger found that conflict is one
of the primary factors. The issues surrounding the conflicts
reflect items from above: pastoral leadership style, finances,
change in worship styles, conflicts among staff, and new
building or renovation.[5]

Chapter 2

The Balancing Act

In this chapter we will explore the second key concept of Bowen Theory—the capacity to differentiate. This concept defines leadership as a matter of how "being" informs and shapes a person's actions.

Human behavior is largely governed by automatic forces. Most of the time, people act without thinking. Differentiation is a process in which a person moves toward a more intentional and thoughtful way of life (and a less automatic way of functioning). Differentiation is the relative ability of people to guide their own functioning by

- thinking clearly
- acting on principle
- defining self by taking a position
- coming to know more about their own instinctive reactions to others
- learning to regulate those reactions
- staying in contact with others
- choosing a responsible course of action

Differentiation is a process that takes place in relationships. It is about balancing two life forces—individuality and togetherness—when interacting with others. As a leader, you will discover that you will always be dealing with the differentiation process and its delicate balance.

Beyond Billiard Balls

Isaac Newton believed that atoms were the smallest bits of matter. They were conceived to be solid, impenetrable elements. Each atom occupied its own space. No atom could get inside another atom; no atom could be reduced to anything smaller. He also contended that all atoms obeyed the same laws. Newton's world was fixed and predictable.

To explain the principles of Newtonian physics, teachers often use the example of billiard balls. They bump into each other, suffer collision, but they cannot connect. They are wholly impervious to one another. Billiard balls knock into each other, but they don't "meet." Like Newton's atoms, the balls are separate, compacted masses always operating according to ironclad laws.

Newton's atomistic model extended beyond physics. It became a paradigm for thinking about society. Individuals were considered to be the atoms of society, and immutable principles and institutions were the means to keep the separate parts intact.[1] Using Newtonian concepts, Freud explained his psychology of relationship. Every person is isolated and impenetrable (unknowable). No one can know another person, but each projects something of him- or herself onto the other. A Freudian psychoanalyst might state, "To myself, I am a self. To others, I am an object. To me, others are objects." According to this viewpoint, people bump into each other like billiard balls, but they don't meet, relate, or commune.

Western medicine has thought atomistically, breaking life into small, isolated parts. Physicians may regard the body as a collection of separate elements. Medical specialists will attend to one body part or section. Several correctives to this way of thinking have emerged. Immunology, once thought to be a system unto itself, is now referred to as *psychoneuroimmunology*, the interaction between brain, other bodily systems, and the immune response. Also, physicians treating patients have begun to pay attention to their own behavior and the patient's sensitivity as part of the treatment process. Addressing physicians, Norman Cousins, who wrote about overcoming a serious illness through the therapy of humor and laughter, urged that when they entered the patient's room to remember the main distance is not from the door to the bed but from the physician's eyes to the patient's. "That distance is best traveled when you bend low to the patient's fear of loneliness and pain and the overwhelming sense of mortality that comes flooding out of the unknown, and when your hand on the patient's shoulder or arm is a shelter against darkness."[2] Cousins envisions the patient to be a "penetrable" person, someone who can be affected by the physician's touch and presence. The patient is not a billiard ball. A physician-patient relationship is essential to treatment.

Western education followed the Newtonian approach, dividing knowledge into discrete parts (reading, writing, and arithmetic). Schools taught "subjects" and had "departments." Students would major in a special field to become expert in one part of knowledge—nutrition, mechanics, optics. Interdisciplinary studies are still rare. Business, too, broke production into assembly lines. Companies structured themselves into subdivisions for sales, research, finance, and production.

Quantum Thinking

About one hundred years ago, quantum physics emerged as the primary model of the physical world. Only recently has it spread into some common ways of thinking. Quantum physics is about the behavior of subatomic particles. Quantum physics, in contrast to Newton's physics, contends there is no world composed of solid, individual parts unaffected by and unrelated to one another. Physicist David Bohm called atomism "the virus of fragmentation."[3] He regarded the idea of fragments and separate, isolated entities as an illusion. When scientists sought to discover the smallest elements, they found particles that were smaller than atoms. These particles became so small that there were no particles—only relationships. Subatomic particles can only come into being because of the presence of other particles. Elementary particles are in essence a set of relationships. They behave as if there is some communication between them. An invisible web of information (a community of coded messages) lies at the core of life.[4] So we will never find a "lonesome lepton" or a "do-it-yourself quark." Or, adapting 17th-century writer John Donne's words, "No photon is an island."

What is true in the world of physics has counterparts in the world of biology. Neurosurgeon Frank Vertosick Jr. argues in his book *The Genius Within* that most living things operate according to the same general model—a *network*. Examples of living networks are ant colonies, immune systems, and brains.[5] The genius of life, therefore, is that life is built of small, discrete things that are connected and interactive. Everything is connected to everything else. All parts are dependent on one another and mutually affect each other.

we're all connected

Emotional Processes

If the environment in which we all live is relational, certainly evidence abounds that the same holds true for the human side of things. "All the 'createds,'" theologian Larry Rasmussen states, "are 'relateds.'"[6] Relationships are played out in what Bowen called "emotional" processes. Bowen gave the concept of "emotionality" a very specific meaning. Emotionality signifies what is instinctual in human behavior, what is imprinted in our nerves as innate, and what embraces the deep biological commands on how to live. He was not alluding to feelings—love, hate, or anger. Although used interchangeably in everyday speech, feelings

and emotions are not synonymous in Bowen Theory. Feelings
are a part of emotional forces, but emotionality refers to all the
processes that guide individuals automatically. The concept of
emotionality addresses what happens when thoughtfulness is by-
passed, when what is not planned and chosen dictates behavior,
when reflexes drive action. Emotionality speaks about reactions
and the interrelatedness of those reactions. Bowen understood
emotional forces as having profound influence upon thoughts,
behaviors, and interactions.

Both *instinct* and *incite* share the same heritage, the Latin
word meaning "to prick" (*instiguere*). Instincts are quick, sudden, and immediate. Through these fast, automatic processes,
the organism and the species confront threats. Automatic forces
provide safety. They have survival value. Strong emotional forces
drive living organisms. They are incredibly sensitive to anxiety
too. At a certain level of intensity, anxiety is adaptive. The sensitivity alerts us to information about the environment, checks
against carelessness, sharpens early awareness, and becomes
motivation for change. However, once anxiety reaches a higher
threshold, its intensity prevents the change anxiety might have
provoked at a lower level. The range of human response is severely restricted. In emotional relationships, a person acts along
a continuum from automatic reactivity and mindlessness to
responsibility and enlightened behavior. We can behave more or
less instinctually or thoughtfully depending on anxiety's effect
on us. Emotional forces drive behavior that is reactive, reflexive,
and defensive.

The Balancing Act

Differentiation describes the process by which two instinctually
rooted life forces—separateness and closeness—are managed by
a person and within a relationship system. In *Family Therapy in
Clinical Practice,* Murray Bowen says, "Differentiation cannot
take place in a vacuum. It has to take place in relation to others."[7]

One can be an individual only in a relationship, and a relationship can function properly only when individuals play distinctive roles in it. Parker Palmer in *The Courage to Teach* summarizes differentiation as embracing "the profoundly opposite truths that my sense of self is deeply dependent on others dancing with me and that I still have a self when no one wants to dance."[8]

Individuality forces are derived from the need to be centered, have a mind of our own, and grow as an emotionally separate human being. Togetherness forces are derivatives of the need to mingle, to be close, to exchange warmth, and to participate in the life of the other. Optimum functioning as a leader would require balancing the two forces, with neither force overriding the other. To live a healthy life requires the capacity to stand apart and to stand together. Sometimes the balance is difficult to achieve because the forces are at odds. The two needs are difficult to meet at the same time. Both of these are very sensitive to anxiety. Such sensitivity may create an imbalance, pushing or pulling a leader to an extreme. Leaders must thread the difficult passage between standing too far away from their followers or blending in too much.

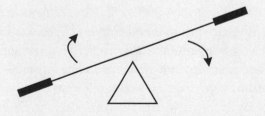

A Loss of Balance

If anxiety about being separate is intense, a person gets too close or too entangled with others. This is *emotional fusion.* If a person's anxiety about being close is intense, he or she gets too disengaged or too remote from others. This is *emotional cutoff.*

Emotional Fusion

Fusion is a word borrowed from physics. It describes what happens when metals are melted together. At a certain temperature, the metals will lose their properties, and they cannot be distinguished one from the other. Emotional fusion happens when people lose their "self." It occurs when one person dominates and the other dissolves into subservience or when both are "nice" to one another to tighten their bond or when each one functions to take care of the other person's feelings. Rainer Maria Rilke described a "fused, muddy communion"[9] as being composed of two "unclarified, unfinished, and still incoherent" people.[10]

Congregations are uniquely vulnerable to fusion. Being idealistic groups, congregations work to maintain high spirits. When premium value is placed on harmony, acceptance, and belonging, people resist information that might disturb their peace. No one wants to speak the truth. If people are emotionally linked, they may not have sufficient space to challenge one another.

"In an anxiety field," Bowen remarks, "the group moves toward more togetherness to relieve the anxiety."[11] More togetherness, however, can distort people's ability to discern and judge. James Surowiecki, author of *The Wisdom of Crowds,* contends, "the more influence group members have on each other, and the more contact they have with each other, the more likely they will believe the same thing and make the same mistakes."[12] Vested in compatibility or likeness, congregations can easily reject differences or information that contradicts their experience. They fear anything that might drive the group apart or alienate someone.

If the community's cohesiveness is strong, their sharing of moods, their behavioral patterns, and even their hot buttons will be alike. It is important to note the difference between giving up self in fusion and giving up self for cooperation or for the community's welfare. Fusion results from *automatic* reactions. Cooperation is *chosen.*

Emotional Cutoff

Rather than standing out from others (differentiation), a person may stand outside of their circle (cutoff). Genuine separateness is differentiation within a relationship, not independence of it. Cutoff is an exaggeration of the need to be separate—"I can only count on myself" or "I'll do it alone." Again, the difference between people who cut off and those who take strong positions is in their functioning. Cutoff is reactive. It's an automatic defense. A well-defined stance is chosen, thought through, and clearly expressed. When cutoff, a person attempts to gain a sense of identity *over against* another person. By projecting a negative label on another ("girlie man," "geek," "chicken hawk"), the person seeks to gain a positive identity for him- or herself. A person defines self against another. Self-definition does not come from one's own center of being. To continue the position of "againstness," the emotional distancer often becomes dogmatic, opinionated, and doctrinaire. In the Bible, the parable of the publican and pharisee praying in the temple illustrates emotional cutoff. The publican prays, "I am guilty." The pharisee prays, "Thank God I'm not like this publican, an adulterer and extortioner" (Luke 18:9–14).

It is wise to remember that whenever someone cuts off from someone significant in their life, the anxiety continues but the awareness of it diminishes. In addition, anxiety not resolved in one relationship tends to be acted out in another one. A lot of displacement happens in relationships.

A Personal Note

"A 'differentiated self' is one who can maintain emotional objectivity while in the midst of an emotional system in turmoil," Murray Bowen says, "yet at the same time actively relate to key people in the system."[13] Differentiation is the capacity to take "I positions" based on principles and to stay connected to others in a responsible way. As a leader, you will experience the differentiation principle in your relationships with others. You will, for instance, want to keep the congregation stable, but not so stable that it lacks energy and forward movement. You will have to contend with some members ready for new ways of seeing and doing things and some riveted to the old. Will your relationship with either side affect your thinking? Will emotional bonds determine your decision, or will your own values and beliefs guide your actions?

A group in the congregation wants you to deal with their frustrations with a staff person. They expect you to take action and either to discipline or to remove the person. You are not convinced of their reasons for such actions or if they have just cause. Will you give in to their wishes to hold on to your friendship with them? Will you take a thought-out position, no matter what?

You are told that the church secretary has embezzled almost $10,000 over the past 18 months. Other leaders believe the revelation of her misdeed would hurt the congregation. They think silence would be the best policy. Your first thought is that the misdeed needs to be communicated to the congregation. Secrets create more harm than knowing the bitter truth. But the other leaders pressure you to go along with the majority viewpoint. Will you relinquish your belief to satisfy the others? Will you stand your ground for openness?

The Leader's Notebook

Undifferentiation/Differentiation Contrast

Crucial to the balancing act is a person's capacity to think clearly, observe, reflect on situations, and base choices and behaviors on principles. The behavior of the poorly defined and the highly anxious person is automatic, emotion driven, and based in the pressure of the moment.

Undifferentiation

(instinctive, reactive, defensive, thoughtless behavior)

1. Accommodates, pleases, or acts to take care of the others' pain

   To maintain a relationship, the leader "gives in" and "gives up" self; is anxious about losing the approval of others.

2. Focuses outside of self

   I do this!

   To stay close to others, the leader pays attention to the actions and feelings of others, not his own. How someone else will react is more important than how he can take a position.

3. Connects emotionally

   To sustain a relationship, the leader reacts to anything that might disrupt or threaten it.

4. Sets vague, nebulous goals

   To have a direction depends on the moment. The climate and goals change with events and moods.

5. Seeks security

   To feel safe, the leader acts cautiously so as not to upset anyone.

Differentiation

(intentional, responsive, responsible, thoughtful behavior)

1. Takes a stand

   The leader works on self-definition based on values; knowing what he believes, the leader takes positions.

2. Focuses on self

   The leader can see how she contributes to a situation; being self-aware, the leader makes changes in her own behavior; has the capacity to step back and see her own interactions with others.

3. Stays connected to others

   The leader relates to others by listening, exchanging ideas, and working toward goals; greater capacity for cooperation and altruism.

4. Sets clear goals

   The leader knows where he is headed; not sabotaged by others' reactivity because he lives with a purpose in mind; stays on course.

5. Seeks challenge

   The leader seeks adventure; she knows that tension stretches a person's growth and stimulates the imagination.

Chapter 3

The Nonanxious Presence

In this chapter we will recognize the powerful influence of a leader's self-regulation in anxious times.

The capacity to self-manage is sometimes referred to as being a "nonanxious presence." Regulating anxiety to the point of having no anxiety is humanly impossible. Anxiety is always present; it is a fundamental human expression, even a healthy response to life. As author Harriet Lerner, in her book *Fear and Other Uninvited Guests,* has jested, to be alive is to have an anxiety disorder.[1]

The nonanxious presence is a description of how a person works to keep the center of control within oneself and as a way to affect relationships in a positive manner. To be a nonanxious presence, you focus on your own behavior and its modification rather than being preoccupied with how others function. In a hospital, a rule for caretakers reads: "In case of cardiac arrest, take your own pulse first."

From Head to Foot

For a long time, people resisted the ideas that mind could move matter, that attitudes could influence molecules, or that faith could play a part in body chemistry. New evidence supports the notions that confidence affects physiological processes and a positive outlook impacts emotional states. Correlation exists between expectations and our physical and emotional condition.

One study, for instance, investigated the influence of thinking on marching. Israeli soldiers were required to make a forced march. They were divided into four groups that were not allowed to communicate with one another. Each group went over the same area on the same day with the same backpack. Group 1 was told the exact distance they had to go (25 miles) and were kept fully informed about how far they had traveled. Group 2 was not told how long the march would be and were not informed regarding the distance they had traveled. Instructed to cover 25 miles, Group 3 was told at the last moment they were expected to march more miles. Meanwhile, Group 4 was told they had to go twice as far as the first group but they were stopped about halfway there. They walked the identical distance, but they walked with different ideas in their heads.

The effects of the march were measured in terms of morale, performance, and change in body chemistry, especially hormones that were believed to elevate as stress mounted. The results:

Group 1   least evidence of stress; highest degree of hopefulness
Group 2   fared the worst in all post-march measurements
Group 3   a very discouraged lot
Group 4   high levels of stress and demoralized

The degree of physiological and psychological stress was determined more by what was in the head of the soldiers than in their tired feet.[2]

Presence and Poise

If groups can be affected by marching orders—clear or confused— congregations can be equally influenced by the steady and calm presence of their leadership. The leader's self-command can stabilize the whole system, despite the pervasive anxiety that exists in and infiltrates the community. In practice, the nonanxious presence of congregational leaders has a positive effect. It leads to less friction, more imagination, and healthier functioning. A person's presence as a leader is incredibly valuable to the welfare of the congregation. How a person handles his anxiety, the anxiety focused on him by others, and the anxiety seeping into the system is vital to the welfare of the congregation. Leadership, often thought to be about action, is more about interaction—that is, regulation of a person's reactivity when relating to others. Since anxiety can be infectious, the leader does not want to be its source or its transmitter. In today's topsy-turvy emotional world, the leader cannot be as anxious as the people she serves. In effect, the anxious leader leaves the congregation without real leadership.

In the biblical story of the golden calf (Exod. 32), anxiety became contagious. By relenting to the peevish demands of the Israelites, Aaron gave them the Prozac of the day. He thought that if he helped them to feel good, they would be contented and their lot improved. Essentially, Aaron succumbed to the pressure of the moment. Aaron joined the excited mob with such haste that he did not in any way calm the emotional uprising. He simply could not tolerate their pain. In contrast, when Moses returned and saw the glittering idol they had constructed, he took a stand. He had the gold melted and pulverized.

A Way of Being

The nonanxious presence is an anomaly, never a full-blown reality. It is intended to be a description of a way of being, the capacity to

- manage our own natural reactions;
- use knowledge to suppress impulses and control automatic reactions;
- keep calm for the purpose of reflection and conversation;
- observe what is happening, especially with oneself;
- tolerate high degrees of uncertainty, frustration, and pain;
- maintain a clear sense of direction.

People have the dual capacity to act without thinking (reactivity) and to take time for thought before they act (response). They cannot, however, control their original impulses, even their first perceptions and impressions. They can control their expression in word or action.

In the Bible, there are numerous instructions about being a nonanxious presence:

> Be angry but do not sin (Eph. 4:26, RSV).
> Grieve, but do not grieve as one who has no hope (1 Th.
>   4:13, author paraphrase).
> In thinking be mature (1 Cor. 14:20, RSV)
> Have no anxiety about anything (Ph. 4:6, RSV).

The nonanxious person is what Paul has in mind when he writes, "Do not repay anyone evil for evil" (Rom. 12:17) and "Bless those who persecute you; bless and do not curse them" (Rom. 12:14). He lists self-control as one of the "fruits of the Spirit" (Gal. 5:23). The writer of Proverbs compares a person without self-control to a city broken into and without walls (Prov. 25:28).

Of Jesus himself, it was said; "When he was abused, he did not
return abuse; when he suffered, he did not threaten" (1 Pet.
2:23). If someone offends us, Jesus commanded that we walk a
second mile or turn the other cheek.

Quick or Deliberate Action

Reactivity is necessary for survival. But we also have the potential
to stop and think—and then act. Both reactivity and response
have advantages. Reactivity's advantage is there is no hesitation.
Act now, think later. Reactivity does the "quick and dirty" work.
Response provides the advantage of time so we can think before
acting. This, however, is extremely difficult amid stress and pressure. We feel an instinctive push for a fast relief of stress.

The nonanxious presence responds (exercises thoughtfulness), instead of reacting (not thinking about anything); that
is, response, not reaction, informs and shapes our behavior.
Under conditions of extreme anxiety, most people become an
anxious presence, lacking restraint and acting on impulse. The
over-excited sympathetic nervous system can cause the body to
collapse, the mind to dwindle in effectiveness, and feelings to
spill over the banks and flood. At the same time, an adrenaline
surge sweeps over the body. Once it floods the brain, our attention is focused solely on the threat. We concentrate narrowly
on something and are unable to process other stimuli or to shift
attention. When obsessing about danger, our capacity to see or
hear other information is nearly impossible. However, the person
who can more readily control anxiety is always more aware of its
presence. To be a nonanxious presence means to acknowledge
anxiety but not let it be the driver of behavior. Being aware of it,
a nonanxious person says to herself: "Anxiety is there. Yet, now
it is where I can see it. I can keep an eye on it. I won't let it slip
back into unconsciousness. With anxiety upfront, I can tame
and harness it. While I may feel like losing it with someone, I
choose not to submit to my instincts. I have good access to my

thinking facilities. My emotional state is not in overdrive. I'll survive this; I can take the sting out of anxiety and be a calming agent."

With this kind of thinking, a leader can bring more imaginative approaches to bear upon the congregation. The leader is not in the clutches of tunnel vision and the instinctive forces of self-preservation.

Stories of Self-Managing Leaders

The influencing potential of the nonanxious presence is not to be confused with being "cool" or being "nice." Nor is it to be construed as denying anxiety in ourselves, as if unaffected by events. The nonanxious presence involves engagement, being there and taking the heat if need be, witnessing the pain, and yet not fighting fire with fire. The nonanxious presence means we are aware of our own anxiety and the anxiety of others, but we will not let either determine our actions. Obviously this means that we have some capacity to tolerate pain both in ourselves and in others.

Crossing Antarctica

The example of Sir Ernest Shackleton epitomizes the concept of the nonanxious presence. Shackleton, an early 20th-century explorer, led an expedition to complete the first overland crossing of Antarctica. Setting sail on the ship *Endurance* on December 5, 1914, 28 men took the risk to battle some of nature's harshest conditions. The crew suffered unbearable situations almost the entire 634 days they were gone. They had no communication with the rest of the world. Whether they were dead or alive, no one knew. They endured brutal cold and ice. At times, their hunger touched the borders of starvation. Then, 327 days into the expedition, the *Endurance,* squeezed between huge blocks of ice, was crushed. Frank Worsley, the captain of the ship, noted in his diary: "We had lost our home in that universe of ice. We had been cast out into a whole wilderness that might indeed prove to be our tomb."[3]

The men saved what they could from the ship to survive. Soon they were confronting not only the forces of a hard environment but also their own human nature—boredom, paranoia, physical exhaustion, and other manifestations of psychological weariness. According to Worsley, their leader, Sir Shackleton, exhibited a "calm, confident, and reassuring" presence. Its effect? In his diary Worsley wrote two citations about Shackleton's presence and its impact on the group: the "leader's state of mind is naturally reflected in the whole party" and "had effects on the attitudes and behaviors of the troops."[4] Sitting on a small piece of ice, buffeted by piercing wind and threatened by chunks of colliding ice, Shackleton himself remembered his feelings: "I confess I felt the burden of responsibility sit heavily on my shoulders; but on the other hand, I was stimulated and cheered by the attitude of the men"—the cross-pollinating effect of the nonanxious presence.[5] Miraculously, all of the members of the expedition survived. The nonanxious leader can broadly affect the entire emotional field. It's as if the leader's calm, reflective demeanor becomes an antibiotic warding off the toxicity of reactive behavior.

Confronting an Abuser

A similar picture of a leader's self-management is seen in the story of St. Paul's Church located in Bristol, a growing town in the shadow of a technology boom. New jobs and houses are attracting a rapid influx of residents. St. Paul's has benefited from the expansion, increasing its membership from five hundred to eight hundred in only two and a half years. With more resources in hand, St. Paul's is adding facilities and staff. To meet the needs of its growing youth population, Bristol has installed a temporary building for young people's activity. Brad, 32 and single, is hired as the youth director. To all, he seems to be an ideal choice, even though he had only been a member at Bristol for five months. But his volunteer work with teens in those months brought extra excitement. Dispensing with a search process, the pastor urged the congregation to offer the position to Brad. He had already captured the support of the youth and their parents.

Seven months after Brad's hiring, Brad and Pastor Drew were invited to the bishop's office in the city. Once there, the bishop acknowledged that Brad's reputation in youth ministry was becoming known. He informed him, however, that he had received information from the Midwest that Brad was wanted there for questioning in the disappearance of his former girlfriend. Brad lightly brushed off the information, saying the old girlfriend was framing him. He had come to the Northwest to start afresh and had found "a wonderful home and a true soul friend in Pastor Drew." The bishop asked Brad to resign. Meanwhile, Pastor Drew, who respected the bishop but doubted Brad's involvement in the case, suggested that they contact Aubrey Wise, the congregational president who worked only a few blocks away from the bishop's office. The bishop agreed but again requested Brad's resignation.

Waiting for Aubrey to arrive, they took a break. Alone, Brad reiterated his defense to Drew, who said nothing. Aubrey arrived, and they reconvened; he was informed of the bishop's request for Brad's resignation. Infuriated that the bishop didn't believe Brad's claim, Aubrey attacked the bishop, charging him with self-interest for fear of a lawsuit, having no concern for the congregation, and prematurely judging Brad. Unmoved by the outburst, the bishop said that he had made the best decision for the congregation and Brad. Eventually Aubrey proposed a compromise, suggesting that Brad take a leave of absence for some weeks and the congregation be told he had to return home to attend to personal matters. The bishop would not agree to the pretense. He again requested Brad's resignation. With reinvigorated anger, Aubrey said that if Brad resigned, he would too. For the next ten minutes, Aubrey told the bishop how his wife, after many years, finally left her childhood church (which he said was a weird group) because their two boys had become active at Bristol through Brad's influence. He solidly supported Brad.

The bishop noted Aubrey's appreciation of Brad, expressed hope that his sons and his wife would continue to be active at Bristol, and acknowledged that Brad's departure would be a significant loss for Aubrey himself. Nonetheless, he continued to ask for Brad's resignation, mentioning that he could not divulge much information, except to say, contrary to Brad's defense that a spurned girlfriend wanted revenge, that the information came from a reliable source. Still claiming innocence, Brad agreed to resign, asking for a six-month severance package and an agreement to confidentiality. Aubrey, muttering disdain and slamming the door, left the room.

On Sunday Pastor Drew announced that Brad had resigned. No reasons were given. By now rumors and gossip had multiplied. Aubrey resigned his position. All kinds of messiness followed, and Bristol ended up losing approximately 125 members in a four-month period. Aubrey and other supporters of Brad actively recruited people to leave. In six months, Pastor Drew departed, never being able to confront the terrible tension. He took an administrative post at a church agency directed by his brother-in-law. Brad received only half of the severance he had requested, but Aubrey and others supplemented the package. Brad disappeared but stayed in contact with several people. Later a report came to the congregation's leadership that Brad was wanted for questioning about assault and battery. His old girlfriend was living in seclusion to escape his physical abuse of her.

The bishop came to the congregation to explain what he could and to field questions. With blistering anger, some people assailed the bishop, who listened attentively and refrained from counterattacking. At the conclusion, several apologized to the bishop for their fellow members' verbal attacks.

Driving back to the city, the bishop told his assistant, who had accompanied him, that he saw signs of a few people coming to terms with the situation. The assistant agreed but thought their number was low. "How do you do it?" the assistant asked. "I couldn't take it." After a brief silence, the bishop responded, "I've learned that I cannot let other people's behavior determine mine."

A Personal Note

In any emotional system, automatic forces will be strong. They are intended to be powerful. They provide safety and ensure survival. That's precisely why our reactions to any kind of threat will be defensive. But we know that reactivity (defensiveness) will excite counter-reactivity from other people. At some point, we have to make a nonanxious response to break the cycle.

John Gottman, who has done extensive research about why some marriages succeed and some falter, offers several helpful insights about human relationships. He found that couples, in both successful and not successful marriages, fall into the cycle of reactivity. Their conversations become a volley of accusations. Before long, the conversation escalates into a blazing argument. The difference, however, between the couples who remain together and the ones who separate is that the successful couples stop the cycled argumentation sooner—that is, before it erupts into complete loss of self-control. The nonsuccessful couples get wrapped up in their own automatic reactions to one another and keep the vicious cycle going. Of course, we know that it isn't only couples who engage in these contentious quarrels. Given sufficient anxiety, people in any relationship can allow automatic forces to rule the day.

Gottman has also learned in his research that how a conversation begins can determine how it ends. If a conversation starts harshly, chances are high that reactivity will conclude it. The harsh startup sparks strong emotionality, which is often difficult to turn down or to turn off. Leaders, of all people, need to see what part self plays in automatic reactions and to control their part. It takes a disciplined effort to manage self: to step back for the moment, observe clearly, select a response, act on principle, and keep a course of direction.[6]

© Ray Johnson. Reprinted with permission.

The Bible speaks about self-control. It is implied in the apostle Paul's description of love—it is not "arrogant or rude" and "does not insist on its own way" (1 Cor. 13:4–5). But our natural instinct is to fire back in defense to an attack. When dealing with reactive people who are attacking us, remember that explaining, justifying, or any verbal defending will simply add fuel to the fire. The attack will be reinforced by our own automatic defenses. I have also learned personally that withdrawing and blaming will have the same effect.

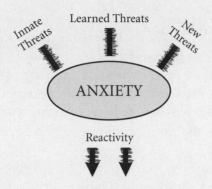

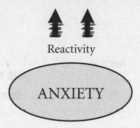

Thoughtlessness   Defensiveness   Automatic Behavior

Reactivity

ANXIETY

Explaining   Justifying   Defending   Blaming   Withdrawing

To be less defensive and automatically reactive to the attacks of others requires some discipline. Nonanxious responses include:

- being thoughtful before acting
- staying calm and poised
- using I statements
- maintaining awareness of self
 focusing on larger purposes rather than winning an argument
- asking questions

Instead of matching reactivity with reactivity, the leader works on a more chosen, deliberate response, one not driven by anxiety.

The Leader's Notebook

Self-Management

To work on your capacity to regulate your own anxiety and reactivity—to be a nonanxious presence—think about these things:

1. Knowing your limits and the limits of others
   a. A clear understanding of where "I" end and someone else begins
   b. A respect for the rights of others to be the way they are, yet refusing to allow others to violate or intrude upon your own rights
   c. A readiness to define who you are from within, rather than adapting to please others or defining yourself over against others

2. Having a clarity about what you believe
   a. Having a set of convictions, values, and beliefs
   b. Knowing what you would "die for" and what's important
   c. Recognizing about what you are certain and about what you are not certain

3. Taking stands with courage
   a. Defining where you stand and what you believe in the face of disapproval
   b. Refusing to give in for the sake of harmony when it is a matter of principle
   c. Standing firm in the face of strong reactions (such as, "You can't think, act, or feel that way and be part of this community!")

4. Staying on course

a. Resolving to follow through, in spite of reactive opposition or sabotage
b. Exercising emotional and spiritual stamina to follow a vision, not allowing reactive forces to change your course.

5. Staying connected to others, despite it all
   a. Maintaining a nonreactive presence with people who are reacting to you (by verbally attacking you, avoiding your presence, minimizing your viewpoint)
   b. Resisting your own impulse to attack or cut off from those reacting to you, or to appease them to dispel their anger or frustration
   c. Managing your own anxiety, not others' anxiety

PART 2

THE LEADER'S FUNCTIONING

After reviewing more than one hundred reports I had prepared for troubled congregations, five recurring issues emerged: (1) *high anxiety;* (2) *systemic impasse* (two parties polarized); (3) *lack of a clear sense of mission* (even if a mission statement was in place, it did not inform their action, and most people were unaware of it); (4) *poor boundaries* (including gossip, allowing hearsay to represent fact, intimidation of others, misuse of funds, voting irregularity, not confronting questionable behavior, indiscriminate firing of staff); (5) and *avoidance of problems.* Whether congregations turned things around or addressed their situation depended on the response of the congregational leadership. Did the leadership focus on the damage or did they look for ways to improve and modify actions? Were they counting the cost or casting the future? Were they on the side of challenge or comfort?

In part 2 of this book, you will discover how significant your functioning as a leader is as you respond to conditions in your congregations, especially in handling emotional reactivity, addressing boundaries, offering clarity, and using conflict as an opportunity for learning and growth.

Chapter 4

Holy Tissue

In this chapter we will study how the brain affects our behavior.

Remarkable studies taking place in neuroscience are making it clear that the brain is the largest secreting organ in the body. It affects not only thinking but also every aspect of our functioning. Knowing about brain functioning can help us understand our own behavior. It will also add to our understanding of what it means to be created in the image of God (*imago dei*)—a responsible and responsive being. The brain is a relationship organ that enables each of us to be an intentional, intimate, and thoughtful self.

Instinctive Living

The life of a lizard is simple. Lounging on a log, the lizard's tongue flicks at a crawling insect. The insect is gone. The lizard doesn't pause to think about whether it is lunchtime yet. There is no question about whether the insect is clean enough to devour. Lizards don't worry about calories or carbs. They don't lightly shake grains of salt on the insect or dip it into cocktail sauce. They just eat. The lizard has nothing to decide, nothing to remember, nothing to learn, nothing to be anxious about, nothing to prepare for. Instinct handles it all.

At times humans will function at the instinctual level of a lizard. As I was writing, my wife quietly entered the room, startling me. "Oh!" I exclaimed. "You scared me!" Why would I be frightened in the safe context of my own home? If my wife's sudden entrance can send me into a reptilian regression, what about a far greater threat, like being surprised by a stranger in an unfamiliar place?

Deeply wired into our protoplasm is a survival mechanism. The Creator has made all creatures with a powerful drive for self-preservation. Whenever we sense that our life is at risk, whenever we imagine a threat, whenever we suddenly feel vulnerable—we react. It's automatic, reflexive, and mindless. The will to survive is incredibly powerful. Brains are designed to react to threats, not to meditate on them. When faced with a challenge to our well-being, rapid reactions take over.

The Alarm System

Early in life we begin to distinguish what is strange and threatening from what is familiar and comforting. Friend or foe? Pain

51

or pleasure? For us or against us? Recessed in the most primitive part of the brain lies the amygdala (*uh-MIG-da-la*), a cluster of cells the size of a grape. The amygdala serves as an early warning signal for danger, constantly scanning the environment for information about what might bring us harm, pain, or injury. Linked to the sensory system, it is ready to blast off an alarm to the brain stem that will set off the automatic reactions of fight, flight, or freeze. In *The Tending Instinct,* UCLA psychology professor Shelley Taylor notes that women often react to stress with the instinct to "tend and befriend."[1] Once the alarm is sounded, the body's stress-response system is activated, bringing changes in blood pressure, a rapid increase of the heartbeat, and a quick release of hormones. The chameleon dashing across the driveway or the deer sprinting into the woods has an amygdala no different from our own. Going on danger alert, the amygdala sends a message to the motor centers of the brain. We jump, tremble, scream, run, stand still, or hold our breath. Our nervous system is hardwired toward survival.

The amygdala also keeps us out of harm's way when there isn't time to think. Escape first, ask questions later. Since the amygdala promotes rapid processing of sensory data, its strength is quickness, not accuracy. It simply can't take time to deliberate and mull over the details of the moment. This primitive brain must operate in a yes-or-no fashion. It's this or that, safe or dangerous, one or the other. It also relies on generalizations and stereotypes to do its urgent and rapid work.

The amygdala also has no sense of time. If a stimulus provokes the fear response early in life, that stimulus is registered in our memory bank. The event is circled and redlined. If the stimulus repeats itself later in life, the same reaction occurs. For example, when I was three-and-a-half years old, Mrs. Magnuson's German shepherd worked itself loose and entered our yard. From time to time, my older brothers and I taunted the dog, but always with a wire fence between us. This time my brothers escaped into the house. Being slower, I climbed a quince tree, hanging onto a limb where I couldn't be harmed.

Still, my heart was pumping fast, and my amygdala was on high terror alert (moving from orange to red). Traumatized for 10 to 12 minutes before an adult retrieved the barking dog, I had an emotional memory stamped forever in my amygdala, because the amygdala keeps score. For the first three years of life, it is the primary site for memory, later transferring this function to the hippocampus.

Our survival training is not something we can usually recall. We merely act it out. Today, if I see a German shepherd, my body freezes.

Losing Proportion

In studies of people whose amygdalae are active, researchers have found that the subjects' memory systems have been affected in two ways: (1) less information about their immediate environment and what is happening is available to them; (2) the pool of objects that resemble the original stimulus is much larger. Threat assessment deteriorates with the triggering of the amygdala. A minor comment is perceived as a major insult. Benign details suddenly take on an emotional urgency. Things are out of proportion. Perception is lopsided or truncated.

When we are flooded with anxiety, we can neither hear what is said without distortion nor respond with clarity. Bruce McEwen, a neuroendocrinologist, comments that stress limits our repertoire of responses. Fixated on what is endangering us, we forfeit our imaginative capacities. We act with a small and sometimes unproductive repertoire of behaviors. With fewer alternatives, we act foolishly. When the amygdala is in control, our perception warps measurably. Our mind is set in imaginative gridlock, we obsess about the threat, and our chances of changing our thinking are almost nonexistent. Reactive forces rule.

Anxiety is built into the nervous system for the sake of preserving the organism and the species. Without it, we are utterly vulnerable. When the amygdala is removed from an animal or is damaged, the animal's behavior changes. Aggressive monkeys become passive. Likewise, mice will amble near cats with no fear. In the book of Isaiah, the prophet refers to the peaceable kingdom where the lion and the lamb lie down next to each other—quite possible if their amygdalae are muted.

Mindset

At Temple Congregation, it seemed as if the leaders synchronized their amygdalae. If Rolf Bach became anxious, you could be sure Carlos Hernandez would be. If Carlos expressed dread, surely Mindy Williams and Nancy McDaniels would follow suit.

The major trigger of anxiety among these leaders was money. No meeting of the leaders passed without money worries. The one exception was Chip Haynes, a new member of the board. He was a realist who thought we do what we can with what we have. But the others had been through almost five years of nagging deficit spending. They couldn't accept the fact that their offerings reached the top five years ago and were steadily declining. Chip suggested that they cut the budget according to receipts and no longer have a line of credit at the local bank.

What Chip did not know was the situation that led to the downturn in giving. This very group of leaders—Rolf, Carlos, Mindy, and Nancy—had blocked an attempt to turn one of the two traditional worship services into a contemporary one. About forty members left as a result of this emotional struggle. Ever since that time five years ago, the offerings had declined. So when Chip offered not only a bit of realism but also a number of suggestions to reverse the giving trends, the others did not respond. Chip was baffled. Seeking to empower the congregation with well-thought options, Chip anticipated at least some discussion. The other leaders, who had come up with only one option in five years (a line of credit at the bank), were unresponsive.

When anxiety prevails, what is most needed is often what is most lacking—namely the imaginative capacities of the people who are leading the congregation. Chip finally learned about the worship "war." He was utterly amazed at how these leaders tried to fund everything as if the former members had never left. Chip—always the realist—encouraged the other leaders to rethink their positions. "You made a decision five years ago," Chip remarked, "and the consequences hurt, even today." He told them the past couldn't be changed but the future could be developed. "Are we going to stay focused on difficulty," Chip asked, "or are we going to look at the possible?" Chip was able to offer options because his inner alarm system had not been affected by the decision made five years ago, which led to a significant loss of giving.

How and How Long

Our fear system can make us too sensitive to danger, diminishing our mental judgments. If called upon too frequently, the body's capacity to adapt to pressure wears down many bodily systems. Under acute conditions, stress protects. But when chronically activated, anxiety can produce not only numbness in thinking but also disease. In studies of police officers, paramedics, and combat veterans, researchers discovered that people in these professions experienced trauma in different ways from one another. The greatest predictor of whether people developed physical or emotional symptoms as a result of their trauma work was *how* they became terrified and *how long* they remained terrified. The intensity and duration of the event were the major factors in stress-related illness. It is no wonder that five years of worry took some toll on the leaders of Temple Congregation, especially when their decision about worship led to the exodus of forty members and a downturn in offerings. They felt responsible for the congregation's nagging financial problems.

On occasion the amygdala will take the "high road" rather than the "low road." Instead of sending signals to the brain stem for quick action, the amygdala directs its signal to the cortex, the thinking brain. The route of the high road provides us with the advantage of time. We can think and look for alternatives. Our thoughts are more precise, accurate, and clear. The cortical thinking brain will not rely on first impressions, act on impulse, or react instantaneously. With the thinking brain in charge, we can be intentional rather than instinctive, responsive instead of reflexive, adaptive rather than defensive, proactive instead of reactive. Of course, the potential always exists for a neural tug of war. The primitive and advanced systems can tussle to achieve control. We are caught between our prefrontal cortex trying to make sense of what is happening and our amygdala sending signals to arouse our emotions. In order for an organism to survive in the long term, it will eventually need contributions from the left prefrontal cortex, so that thoughtful approaches rather than instinctive ones guide behavior and decisions.

The Human Part

The left prefrontal cortex houses our humanity. It is the brain region just behind the eyes that integrates information and inhibits emotional impulses that rise from the amygdala. The left prefrontal cortex is fully developed only in humans. It is crucial for all higher-order, purposeful behavior. Neuroscientist Alexandr Luria has called this region of the brain "the organ of civilization." His student Elkhonon Goldberg has referred to it as the "executive brain."[2] If it is impaired, we lose hindsight, insight, and foresight. We function with fewer social constraints. We express less responsible behavior. From medical history, we have learned about the case of Phineas Gage—a promising, young railroad foreman in Vermont who, through a bizarre accident, had his left prefrontal cortex severely damaged. A responsible, mild-mannered, and sociable person, he was transformed into an irresponsible loudmouth and an irritable individual. His physician remarked: "Phineas Gage is no longer Phineas Gage."[3]

William Shakespeare lyricized the whole brain as the "soul's frail dwelling-house."[4] Now some neuroscientists locate sacred-

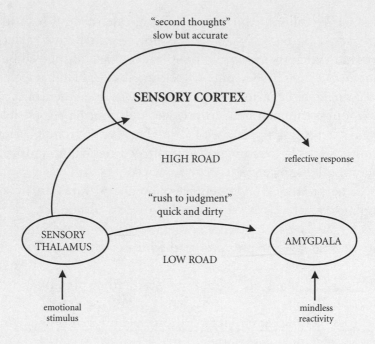

Figure 4.1
The low road has the advantage of speed and simplicity. The high road provides accuracy and precision.

ness more precisely in the left lobes, which house the left prefrontal cortex. "'If God speaks to man, if man speaks to God,'" neuroscientist Candace Pert observes, "'it would be through the frontal lobes.'"[5] In her book about the brain, *The 3-Pound Universe,* author Judith Hooper quotes Pert: "'I'm learning that the brain obeys all the physical laws of the universe. It's not anything special. And yet it's the most special thing in the universe.'"[6] Paul MacLean, another neuroscientist, refers to the left prefrontal cortex as "the angel lobes."[7] Without the left prefrontal cortex, humans would function just like another animal, letting instinct handle life. A nightmare scenario would ensue: creatures pitted against each other in a struggle for survival.

I refer to the left prefrontal cortex as "holy tissue." The Hebrew word for "holy" (*kadosh*) can signify what is special or

unique. To call something holy is to indicate that it is set aside
for sacred purposes. Without this holy tissue, a civil society
would never form. We could bond for the sake of survival but
not for purposes beyond our own self-interest. Rather than being
goal-directed, behavior would be unpredictable and arbitrary.
Without a left prefrontal cortex, we could not be responsible
beings, reflecting the image of God. The left prefrontal cortex
prospers life. It gives us special gifts to create, enjoy, and find
meaning in being alive.

The prefrontal cortex enables humans to function in six
unique ways:

1. Humans can project into the future:

    • Humans are capable of predicting, planning, and
      hoping.
    • The left prefrontal cortex is the only part of the brain
      with a sense of the future.
    • Animals stay in the instinctual moment, but humans
      can anticipate.
    • A sense of the future endows humans with the capacity
      to find purpose and meaning in life.
    • Without the capacity of the left prefrontal cortex,
      there would be no hope, no resurrection, essentially
      no Christian faith.

2. Humans can exercise social competence:

    • Humans can see beyond themselves and their own
      self-interest.
    • We can obtain the feeling required for identifying
      with another person, making possible the insight to
      plan for the needs of others as well as ourselves, and
      making love possible.

- We can express positive regard and compassion.

3. Humans can observe self and environment:

   - We can stand back from experience and be conscious of it.
   - We are self-reflective.
   - We learn from experience by studying ourselves.
   - We can look inward to discover what is happening in the outside world (a dog knows a lot but doesn't know it knows a lot).

4. Humans can use imagination:

   - We can picture different scenarios.
   - We create possibilities.
   - Imagination releases us to "paint outside the lines."
   - Imagination develops options, drawing attention to the unusual.

5. Humans can think critically:

   - We weigh issues.
   - We judge.
   - Humans problem solve.
   - We use principles to guide behavior.
   - We employ meaning to modify innate tendencies.

6. Humans can regulate emotional forces:

   - We can quiet an excited amygdala.
   - We can consciously cool down reactive, impulsive forces
   - We can exercise self-control.

- Humans can self-monitor, providing internal supervision.
- We manage sensory input.

Despite these unique capacities, the lower brain can hijack the frontal lobes. When we are apprehensive, we can use imagination to create bogus threats. Worrying beyond reason, we can conjure up a series of terrifying "What ifs?" If mobilized into the service of the reactive brain, the frontal lobes can produce all kinds of defensive reasoning. When we rationalize our behavior to defend ourselves, our thinking brain is now at the command of the reacting brain. Rationalizing is defensive behavior. All defensiveness originates in the lower, survival brain.

Consider the inventory of horrible things we might imagine. We don't need lions, witches, or dark holes to frighten ourselves. Once we are conditioned to fear something, even if imaginary, our fear can gain a life of its own. The assumptions of the lower brain are hard to reframe. Author Harriet Lerner notes in *Fear and Other Unwanted Guests* that she wishes she could be like her cat Felix, who feels fear only when fear is due.[8]

Branches and Vines Congregation had a history of poor relationships with its denomination's judicatory, the regional office that has oversight responsibility. When congregational leaders had to confront tension among Branches and Vines staff, they hesitated to notify the judicatory staff, much less seek their advice. They feared the judicatory would try to eliminate the senior pastor because he had irresponsibly stirred up the judicatory staff's animosity toward him. The congregation's leaders had the notion that the judicatory was "after him." The senior pastor had fed their fear, falsely accusing judicatory staff of being cold bureaucrats and inept. In reality, most of the congregations in the area envisioned the judicatory leadership as fair and capable individuals. The thinking capacities of the whole Branches and Vines leadership team had been captured by imaginary fears. If they had researched the work of the judicatory, they would have discovered that the information they were given did not match the reality of a competent judicatory staff.

Beyond Survival

Healthy functioning of the left prefrontal cortex is the best hope for a sane and safe world, as well as for a healthy congregation. It is the organ that enables each of us to be a responsible and responsive person, to be self-aware and thoughtful of others, indeed a reflection of the image of God. In the absence or impairment of the left prefrontal cortex, the amygdala romps around like a two year-old, principles are not in place to guide behavior, and a sense of hope is lost.

The brain is an incredible instrument, but whether it is at the service of a chronically anxious person or a reflective person makes a world of difference. Notice that when Jesus taught people, he directed his energy to their left prefrontal cortex, not the amygdala. He sought to reach people thoughtfully, not reactively. He told stories; he asked questions. He spoke about the future. He respected and noticed those who came to him. Jesus clearly stated his position and defined himself. Both Jesus's invitation to trust God's unconditional love and the instruction on loving action are designed to free us from our survival brain with its defensive instincts, self-serving protective behaviors, and reflexive reliance on aggression. Could we imagine Jesus saying to us:

> Come, let go of all your survival schemes, and follow me. Do you think an eye for an eye is better than a new way of seeing? Can you become as a little child again, the way you were before you learned all your self-protective reactions? Do you think your survival strategies are long-lasting? Don't they last for the moment but not the long run? Doesn't the lower

brain play it safe? Doesn't it like repetition and precedence? It won't shake habits. Can you risk yourself, throw yourself to the winds, and drop your defenses? Will you use your "holy tissue" to do the work that is holy—being set apart to lead my people?

A Personal Note

Survival instincts make sense when dangers are real. By doing threat assessment and sending an alarm, the amygdala serves as a protective device. A person with an impaired amygdala is in grave danger. The person is unable to evaluate whether or not a situation is dangerous. Sometimes, however, the amygdala is not injured but it fails to recognize potential or impending danger. Let me illustrate from my consulting work with congregations.

Whisper Valley Congregation invited me to help them with the sticky problem of their senior pastor. The primary issue was his deception and dissembling. Fourteen of sixteen staff members asked for his removal. One of his supporters, a devout and active member of the church, defended the senior pastor against the charges. When the evidence of the pastor's lying was presented, the defender dismissed it lightly. I was baffled because this person was the head of the legal department of a major corporation. Only later did I discover that his wife had been the chairperson of the search committee that brought the current senior pastor to Whisper Valley. Again and again, he would mention that the senior pastor fit the desired profile better than any candidate they had interviewed a couple of years ago. Fitting the profile, however, had nothing to do with the pastor's deceitful behavior. Perhaps the involvement of the defender's wife in the search process led him to consider the senior pastor as a nonthreat. His amygdala gave no signal of alarm. He dismissed the lying as inconsequential. Others, however, saw the pastor's deceit as harmful, even abusive.

We are not alarmed by the same things. If we see a tiger in the wild, for instance, anxiety is elicited immediately. If we see a tiger in a zoo, we are fascinated. Sandy Harris, a cheerful and loving pastor of Westbank Church, had been warned on a number of occasions that her secretary was speaking out of turn—meaning she gossiped and revealed confidential information. Emily had served as Sandy's secretary for nearly four years and had become a close confidant. "That's not the Emily I know," she repeated to herself. Not until Sandy's brother reported an incident involving Emily's careless and harsh talk about a member did Sandy take notice of Emily's behavior.

As much as we need an active amygdala to warn us of danger, we likewise need the left prefrontal cortex to put a check on it. Imagine the havoc we would encounter if the amygdala had no inhibitor on its alarm signals. With each anxious "beep," we would automatically assume the defensive position and react. We would be chronically anxious. The survival brain would be totally in charge of our lives. If anything threatened our viewpoints, we would instinctively reject it.

Early in my consulting work, I made the mistake of thinking that if I presented issues to a congregation clearly, the people would respond appropriately. What I discovered is that not all people in a given situation will find clarity comforting. Even if the information is quite clear, if it runs contrary to someone's viewpoint, they will contest it. Their own emotionality overrides their thinking capacity. Their emotionality limits the thinking brain's capacity to focus on the facts. The survival brain will protect us not only from bodily harm but also from challenges to our world of insight and meaning.

The Leader's Notebook

Thoughtful Action

One of my goals in working with congregations in anxious times is to direct them to a more thoughtful position. Instead of simply accepting their impassioned comments, I am hoping to draw out their capacity to be reflective. In the heat of the moment or early in the process, this is extremely difficult to achieve. The instinct to defend is simply too strong. To move people to their left prefrontal cortex, I have used the following exercise:

1. Describe the current situation. The difficulty is...
   Party 1 would probably say the key issue involves...
   Party 2 would probably say the key issue involves...
2. Describe the ideal situation. I would like to see...
   Party 1 would like...
   Party 2 would like...
3. What has Party 1 or Party 2 done to move the impasse, conflict, or problem toward a beneficial outcome?
   Party 1 did...
   Party 2 did...
4. What outcomes are likely if the impasse, conflict, or problem is managed?
5. What outcomes are likely if the impasse, conflict, or problem is not managed?
6. What, in your view, is preventing movement toward progress, improvement, or change?
7. Is there a third party? How would they answer these questions?

Chapter 5

Influencing the Emotional Field

In this chapter we will see how the position of the leader positively affects the emotional field in anxious times.

By not exercising responsibility at these times, the leader can influence the field in a negative or destructive way. A positive outcome will emerge if the leader's presence and functioning is centered in principle, based on self-regulation, and anchored by taking thoughtful positions. Principle provides clarity; self-regulation helps to avoid extremes; thoughtful positions lead to necessary action.

Emotional Field

A "field" is a region of influence. The field is nonmaterial but happens when matter affects matter; a field is an environment created by its interaction. The paradox of field theory is that a field comes into being when matter draws near matter. If all matter were removed from the universe, there would be no field. But once the field exists, it determines the functioning of the parts more than any part influences the field, even though the presence of the parts is necessary for creating the field.

In an electromagnetic field, currents and waves create a field of force, a distribution of energy in space. In an emotional field, people interact, mutually affecting one another's behavior. A field of force and energy is distributed. Remove people and no field exists. Bring people together and there is interaction, energy, and a region of influence. In an emotional field, people function as they do because of the presence of one another. In a field, particles—people or electrons—will not necessarily function according to their nature, habit, or personality. An aggressive salesperson in business may be a compliant, quiet member in a congregation. The salesperson may be very practical in business affairs, but once in the circle of the church, the salesperson is a mystic. What is important is the individual's *position* within the field. Change a particle's position, and a particle appears to have a different nature. Particles behave as they do because of the presence of other particles and their own position in the field.

Because of the leader's position in an emotional field, the leader affects the whole most significantly. Will the leader make choices based on principle or will the leader choose on the basis of expediency? Will the leader take a clear position or will the leader change sides according to the audience? Will the leader, through a differentiating, nonanxious presence, promote creativity or will the leader's high anxiety encourage reactivity?

Influence

The leader is always in a position to influence the emotional field. The leader's positive influence is most dramatic at times of crisis, bewilderment, stagnancy, and new situations.

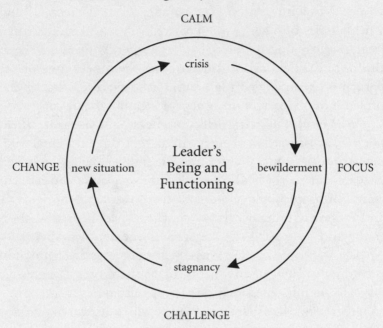

   Looking at each of these critical times in the life of a congregation, we can see what the leader brings to the particular circumstance:

Circumstance	Influence
crisis	calm
bewilderment	focus
stagnancy	challenge
new situations	change

Of course, the leader can maintain or add to a crisis by being reactive instead of responsive. The stagnant congregation can be led by someone who avoids challenge rather than initiates it. When a new situation requires a change, the leader may be the one blocking it.

The leader's positive influence in crucial times is accomplished through both the leader's being (demeanor, spirit, and poise) as well as the leader's thoughtful functioning. Both attitude and action influence outcomes.

Crisis/Calm

Suddenly a crisis develops. The need for the leader's calm reflection and thoughtful action is paramount. At Hardin Memorial Church, Mark Barnes and other lay leaders responded in this fashion during a crisis.

"Have you heard about Everett Shostrom?" Ashley asked her husband, Mark, the chairman of the board of deacons at Hardin Memorial Church. Calling from the hospital where she was visiting, Ashley frantically reported: "Everett has been arrested for beating his wife. They brought Marie here to the hospital. She's in critical condition. Everett's in county jail, according to what Deputy Smith told me." Mark sat motionless in his office chair. "I can't believe it," he muttered.

Mark rushed across the hall to the office of Dennis Rasmussen, also a deacon at Hardin Memorial. The two kept saying, "Anyone but Everett." Dennis called his brother Eric, Hardin's youth minister, hoping to reach him at the church office. Eric, as shocked as the others, said he was coming to Dennis's office.

Everett Shostrom, a quiet man and longtime member of Hardin Memorial, was a well known dentist in the community, respected for his volunteer work with the elderly and his participation in a free clinic for the poor and homeless. No one knew of his violent temper and tendency to abuse. Mark thought about Everett and Marie's two sons in college at Statesville. He

knew that Rev. Acker was on vacation fishing in the wilds of the
Northwest and would be difficult to contact.

When Eric arrived at his brother's office, he recommended
that they call the judicatory's regional director of ministry for
assistance. He also proposed calling Bonnie Nelson, who worked
for the Red Cross and would bring a wealth of experience from
emergency circumstances. By the time Bonnie arrived at Dennis's
office, the report on the street was that Marie was in surgery
but severe brain damage was suspected. Everett was isolated in
a cell, waiting for an attorney to come.

To the credit of all four of the church leaders, they planned
how to handle things, who would be responsible for what, and
when they would reconvene. Eric drove to Statesville College
to minister to the Shostroms' sons. Mark prepared an e-mail to
send to the other deacons of the congregation. Bonnie said she
would contact Rev. Acker, if possible. Dennis called the regional
minister, and Ashley chose to stay with Marie at the hospital.

That evening a prayer vigil was held at Hardin Memorial.
An emergency meeting of the board of deacons met afterwards.
Grief. Anger. Disbelief. Feelings of powerlessness. Some people
expressed guilt, wondering if they had failed Everett and Marie.
Many were asking, "Why?"

Rev. Acker returned late the next day. He and Mark planned
how to continue caring for all parties. Everett was arraigned;
Marie was transferred to the larger city hospital for long-term
care. Michael and Matthew, the Shostroms' sons, went to stay
with their grandparents, dropping out of college for the semester.
Members of the congregation dealt with the shock in different
ways. Later, many reported how calming and healing were the
words and presence of Rev. Acker and Mark Barnes. They praised
Bonnie Nelson for volunteering to take the time to talk to them
in groups and individually.

As the shock began to fade, the sadness lingered because of
Marie's long recovery, Everett's impending trial, and the yellow
crime-scene ribbon surrounding the Shostroms' house—a visual
reminder of the incredible event. Still, the collective calm of the

leaders affected the emotional field. It was not as if Mark, Dennis, Bonnie, or the pastors didn't feel anxious, have doubts, or run the normal range of feelings and questions. Their ability to be thoughtful and decisive in spite of their own nagging anxiety made a difference. At Hardin Memorial, the leaders were not drawn into making anxious "fix it" statements, minimizing what happened, or demanding that people put this behind them. Nor did leaders express an anxious piety to dampen questions about God's purposes and mercy. The leaders allowed the darkness to be, knowing dawn was months away. In one of Rev. Acker's sermons, he quoted what theologian Joseph Sittler called "the germinating darkness," proposing, "If you completely wipe out the darkness, nothing can come forth and grow."

At times of crisis, a congregation functions best when its key leaders are differentiated. The crisis certainly ushers in confusion, despair, and a temporary period of powerlessness and hopelessness. It is a crucial time for the community to slow down and to reflect on what happened. The natural instinct is just the opposite—to press immediately for decisions, explanations, and actions to dispel the awful uncertainty and helplessness. Impatience has its source in anxiety. Experience has taught us that healing has its own timetable. Being hasty is low-road functioning.

During a crisis, a structure of some sort is needed. When things are falling to pieces, the emotional system needs a container—something to hold the parts together, something that promises that chaos is not king. Crisis may shatter our beliefs, threaten our security, and expose our vulnerabilities. To counteract these and other disturbing consequences, leaders, by their patience, hope, and reframing of the event, can calm the people who are affected.

Bewilderment/Focus

Congregations that lack a focus are like a sailor on a lake without a destination. With no port in mind, the sailor will not know how to adjust the sails to guide its course. The sailboat will drift or meander. Congregations not focused on their mission (destination) meander or float aimlessly too.

For 13 years, Sterling Marsh led Boston Church through several natural disasters, a couple of rough spots regarding staff members, and one major conflagration. Now, however, he faced the problem of his own ennui. He wondered if he had worn thin and had lost his influence on the congregation. For almost 12 months, he detected a mood of indifference. People seemed tired. Maybe, Sterling thought, he was projecting his own exhaustion onto them. Approaching his 60th birthday, Sterling did some self-reflection about being worn down. Could this dry period in the congregation be a mere mirror of his own parched soul?

Every year Sterling led a leaders' retreat, and for the last two years he had used Peter Drucker's self-assessment tool for nonprofit organizations to structure the event:

1. What is our mission?
2. Who is our customer?
3. What does the customer value?
4. What are the results?
5. What is our plan?

For the upcoming retreat, Sterling decided to use the same questions but address them in a new way. Maybe, he thought, the new format would evoke new responses. He had the leaders answer the five questions as if they were each of the following people:

- a 15-year-old
- a migrant worker
- a single parent
- a recently widowed 69-year-old
- a new convert
- a parent with teenage children
- a 59-year-old minister not sure if he's on empty

The retreat led to a recognition that the congregation was meandering and that they had become too dependent on Rev. Marsh. How could the missional energy that had waned be re-invigorated? Known for his work on emotional intelligence, science writer Daniel Goleman observes, "Groups begin to change only when they first have fully grasped the reality of how they function."[1] Boston Church's first challenge consisted of seeing the facts of the situation and refocusing in order to mobilize people's energy. Providing a focus is the work of leadership. If the congregation is not focused on its mission, it will focus on something—perhaps the budget, the past glory days, or the pastor's performance.

You may have heard the story depicting three bricklayers working on the same project: The first bricklayer is asked what he is doing. His answer: "I am laying bricks." The second one replies that he is erecting a wall. The third bricklayer says, "I am building a cathedral." In bewildering times, leaders need the third bricklayer's vision: focusing on what might be possible and seeing the opportunity buried in the confusion.

Stagnancy/Challenge

In the biosphere in Arizona, a three-acre greenhouse in the desert, people noticed that fruit was falling off the first trees prematurely. What had happened? Inside this encapsulated environment, wind, a force that challenges the tree's branches and strengthens them, is absent. Without wind the branches do not gain sufficient strength to hold the fruit to the time of maturation.

The leader is the one who can most influence the congregation by challenging it. The leader functions like the wind. When challenging, leaders will surely kick up the dust of anxiety, since resistance is a natural reaction to challenge. Resisters essentially say, "Let us be content in our homeostatic world." A leader has to expect people to raise opposition when the community is resting comfortably, and then it is pushed, pulled, or stretched.

The leader challenges but mostly at a rate people can absorb. Readiness needs to be considered carefully. Some outstanding proposals to challenge congregations have failed only because the opportune time had not really emerged or the challenge did not enroll a sufficient number of people to support its implementation. Merely driven by someone's impulsiveness, the challenge never gained support or momentum.

Opportune times to challenge usually appear when

- the community hits bottom;
- real events open eyes and sharpen awareness;
- a sudden, shattering experience occurs;
- the congregation is in a learning mode and someone excites their attention.

People are not automatically opposed to challenge. Many will respond to it if they consider it worthy of their investment and within the reach of their resources. Stretching is not only good for our muscles but also for the fibers that connect people in a community.

A small congregation in the Midwest accepted the challenge of cosponsoring a Sudanese family of five to settle nearby. They found a house for them, collected furniture, towels, bedding, and whatever was needed to make a house into a home. The father, who could speak English, began working at a hospital. The children were registered in school and regularly tutored by a group of church members. The congregation stretched itself in caring for this new family in town. The father, a delightful person to be around, died suddenly from a mysterious illness, perhaps an infection he picked up at the hospital for which he had no immunity. The necessary support for the family became more than the small congregation and its partner church could handle. Representatives of both congregations sought additional assistance from other congregations. To present their case for additional help, they developed a Bible study based on the book of Deuteronomy. Sometimes called the "neighbor book," it is full of counsel and encouragement to befriend the stranger, who is without advocates and protection (Deut. 10:17–19; Deut 24:17). Then they shared Bible study and their experience with the congregations interested in helping, challenging them to be sponsors.

New Situations/Change

Western society is experiencing a shift from one historic period to another. Many believe no parallel exists in history for the current rate of change. And what shaped past centuries is yielding to a fresh set of ideas and perspectives. For thousands of years, civilizations focused on continuity. The overriding and new fact of history is *living with* constant, radical change. Rapid transformation is becoming a normal way of life. Would you believe Chicago has more Muslims than Methodists? Soon America will have more Muslims than Jews. Some prominent shifts affecting congregations include these:

- People are less interested in an intellectual approach to faith and increasingly drawn to the experience of faith.
- Fewer and fewer people are following in the footsteps of the family's denomination and more are shopping for a church.
- Congregational membership is less organized around an immediate neighborhood area and more around a regional area.
- Authority in the congregation is shifting from vertical dimension (top-down) to the horizontal structure (network, teams).
- People are attracted to churches that offer certainty more than to churches that offer information or knowledge.
- The visual is replacing the verbal as a major avenue for communicating the message the church wants to convey.

- Churches experience greater competition for members. Those that meet the needs of the "consumers" are favored.
- Loyalty to an institution is being replaced by participation in meaningful groups or networks.
- The role of worship is changing from a strengthening of the believer's faith to a way of evangelizing.

Congregations have been and will continue to be affected by swift, broad changes. The church traditions that organized religious identity are waning. New, potent forces are emerging—declining loyalty to denominations, a growing number of people who regard themselves as Christians but are not church affiliated, the generalities of spirituality supplanting the specifics of theology, religion as a feel-good phenomenon instead of a path of sacrificial living. A new social activism is emerging with interest in preventing AIDS, addressing global warming, and feeding the hungry.

Congregations are also affected in other significant ways. "Not only are we entering a millennium of perpetual novelty but also the future promises a continuous escalation in the rate of change," the late rabbi Edwin Friedman observed, "The change will have a significant effect on the emotional processes of all families and other institutions."[2] Friedman foresaw these circumstances creating a chronically anxious state for the immature numbers of society and a condition of permanent stress for all leaders.

Sometimes leaders get into the position of thinking they are primarily responsible for preserving tranquility in the congregation. The last thing they want to do is upset anyone. Consequently, they hide embarrassing information or they avoid making changes that might spark controversy. The leadership position favors "togetherness forces"—that is, the leader feels responsible for keeping the system together, for everyone's happiness and comfort. Anything that might jostle or jar the equilibrium is instantly rejected. The congregation's unity su-percedes anything else. Changes threatening to upset people are prohibited. Instead of leading, the leader pacifies:

> "I'll take care of you . . .
>> so you don't have to hear harsh things."
>> so you don't have to struggle with making a decision."
> "I'll keep the lid on the pressure that threatens to boil over…
>> so you are not forced to think."
>> so you are not emotionally upset."

Friedman noted that when a leader is predominantly a "peac-emonger," a "failure of nerve" follows.

> By [peacemonger] I mean a highly anxious risk avoider, someone who is more concerned with good feelings than with progress, someone whose life revolves around the axis of consensus, a "middler," someone who is so incapable of taking well-defined stands that their "disability" seems to be genetic, someone who treats conflict or anxiety like mustard gas—one whiff, on goes the emotional gas mask and they flit. Such leaders are often "nice," if not charming.[3]

Friedman believed that the antagonism of the anxious is pro-portionate to the niceness of the leader.

If the leader adapts his functioning to the weakest members, he enables their dependency, encourages their happy ignorance, and reinforces their helplessness. To protect a congregation from bad news or upsetting changes is to admit that the system is weak and fragile, too brittle to be challenged. The congregation's threshold for pain is low and its opportunity for changing is negligible.

But distress is not always an obstacle to learning. Pain can be a teacher. Real learning begins when the threat of pain emerges. Everyone has learning anxiety (a general dread of entering unfamiliar territory or exploring new ways of understanding).

The anxiety that spurs growth is survival anxiety, when you choose something new because survival itself is at stake.

If the leader does not have some degree of toleration of pain, it's doubtful that others will be able to tolerate pain and use it for growth. As a result, Friedman asserted, the weakest, most dependent, and most emotionally driven people will control the congregation. They will influence the emotional field, not you.[4]

A Personal Note

Anxiety is the automatic and natural reaction to anything that might threaten a person's safety. As anxiety increases in emotional systems, people's behavior is more automatic. That means people are less thoughtful and imaginative, resistant to whatever signals pain, and generally in an edgy mood.

Whatever the trigger of anxiety might be, whatever the anxious behaviors, the healthier way for leaders to function to affect this emotional field in pain would be to

- recognize resistance as a normal reaction to leadership rather than taking it personally;
- know that relationships are reciprocal and interactive and that our own calm, reflective functioning influences the congregation positively;
- exercise patience because anxiety's effect on an emotional field is immediate, whereas our well-composed functioning influences the emotional system in the longer term;
- consider their goals for the congregation to avoid giving in to the pressure of the moment, such as by quickly fixing problems and taking care of people's anxiety;

- learn to tolerate anxious times in order to use them as opportunities for creative responses;
- manage their own anxiety.

This capacity to step back and think clearly allows you to withstand the urgent, automatic reactions prompted by pain and anxiety, both within yourself and others, brought on by crisis or any of the other three situations. By positioning yourself in this way, you will empower yourself. Your self is the only instrument you have to struggle, comfort, or make peace with others. The more of your self you have at your disposal, the stronger you will be in influencing the emotional field. The prayer of St. Francis (much admired by Murray Bowen), "Lord make us instruments of your peace," is difficult to pray if you are not an instrument in the first place.

The Leader's Notebook

Thinking about Change

- You can never make only one change. Change here creates change there.
- Change arouses the survival instincts.
- No transformation happens without a crisis.
- No significant change in history happened because at first a majority voted for it (Margaret Mead).
- Change, like most things in life, starts small and grows larger.
- "Those who come first are the last to accept new ideas"[5] (Edwin Friedman). This is the paradox of the change agent who, once his or her change is completed, tends to block or stall the new changes someone else wants to implement.

- No emotional system will change unless people in the system change how they function with one another.
- Learning is change. Resistance to the new is stronger if it is less familiar. Resistance to change is less likely if learning adds facts or meanings that do not disturb what is already known.
- Change is stimulated when we look at things from a different angle, associate with new people, pass through a critical moment.
- "Our brain is much better at changing the world than living with that change"[6] (Diane Ackerman).
- "Congregations that systematically avoid conflict are also very likely to avoid change"[7] (Nancy Tatum Ammerman).

Chapter 6

The Essential Edge

In this chapter we will examine the leader's role and responsibility in creating and maintaining healthy boundaries.

The significance of a boundary is disclosed in the creation story of Genesis. In the beginning, there is chaos. The Bible depicts an undifferentiated and unintegrated mass. The story begins: "The earth was a formless void and darkness covered the face of the waters" (Gen 1:2). To bring order, God separates the heavens from the earth, the day from the night, and the land from the sea, creating spaces between things and edges and outlines to define them. Integration happens, too, with the consolidation of the waters and by each creature reproducing only its kind. God creates separate things *and* brings together that which is separate.

The differentiation of creation extends to language. God invites Adam to become a co-creator and to name things. "This is a horse; this is a goat." Literary critic Roland Barthes says that "the founding function of differences . . . is the basis of all language."[1] Words differentiate one thing from another. They provide specificity and distinctions that help us order our world.

Boundaries are necessary for relationships too. The word *existence* comes from a word meaning "stand apart" (*ex-sistere*). Definite boundaries are essential to human identity—the other is truly different from me. Boundaries are also the place where the other and I meet—the essential edge. Only separate entities can meet and connect.

Boundaries provide identification and connection—and protection. A tree is covered with bark to safeguard it against insects, disease, and harsh weather. The atmosphere of the earth is a boundary that shields it from the sun's harmful ultraviolet rays. In ancient times, a city was enclosed by walls to protect its inhabitants. The body's skin is a protective sheath. Wherever a boundary exists in life a relatively stable form of life also is present. In the absence of or injury to boundaries, there is a return to some type of chaos.

Leaders are pivotal in creating and maintaining healthy boundaries, especially in anxious times. Leaders establish clear procedures and processes and secure a safe environment. Theodore Schwenk, a writer about human nature, notes, "Boundaries are the birth places of living things."[2]

Cells and Souls

Discoveries in the field of microbiology reveal that molecules and human beings behave in similar ways. Parallels exist between cellular activity in the body and human interaction. However, Sherwin B. Nuland, clinical professor of surgery at Yale University, observes that "only with caution should a thesis be extrapolated from cells to societies, but sometimes the speculations that follow from witnessing observable natural events are too suggestive to ignore."[3]

We are nature, and the discovery of common principles between cells' behavior and our behavior is not surprising. For instance, cells grow, differentiate, migrate, and influence the behavior of their neighbors, quite like us. In describing the operation of cancer cells, Nuland himself notes how they have an unlimited capacity to grow and to generate new tumors. He compares these cells to "a disorganized autonomous mob of maladjusted adolescents, raging against society from which it springs. It is a street gang intent on mayhem."[4] Physician and science writer Lewis Thomas suggests "the analogy between a city undergoing disintegration and a diseased organism does not stretch the imagination too far."[5] Paul Brand, a medical missionary, claims that the cells in our bodies can teach us about how larger organisms function (families, groups, villages, nations), especially "one specific community of people that is likened to a body more than thirty times in the New Testament . . . the Body of Christ."[6]

The cell is the basic unit of life. The word *cell* derives from the Latin word, *cellelae,* signifying "a small room." By definition, a cell has boundaries. The cell membrane is necessary to mediate exchanges of energy, matter, and information.

As a cell matures, it becomes differentiated, meaning it limits its responses to a single task. The cell specializes, becoming bone, skin, or muscle. While seeking its own goal, the cell cooperates with other cells to create an entity much larger than itself (organelle, organ, organism). Internally the human organism is essentially a society of individual cells cooperating with one another, reflecting separate-yet-connected components. This is precisely the design of mature human relationships—even as they draw close to others, individual selves retain their integrity.

Uninvited Guests

At times in both the human organism and human relationships, the interaction of individual components threatens the well being of the whole. For instance, an infection rarely occurs simply because viruses are present in the human body. Few viruses pose a threat. Pathogenesis (the invasion of infectious organisms) begins when the virus becomes aggressive. Lacking the equipment to replicate on their own, viruses need help from elsewhere. They target certain tissue. Once they find that target, they may fuse with the cell's membrane or burrow their way through the membrane. The resulting infection depends on the interaction between the surfaces of the virus and the host cell. At a conference I attended, physician Sidney Baker asked: "Can you think of any pathology that does not involve a loss of integrity of a surface or boundary?" Lewis Thomas described it this way: "Disease usually results from . . . an overstepping of the line by one side or the other, a biologic misinterpretation of borders."[7]

With infectious disease, the virus and the host cell have become chummy. To complete an infectious cycle, a virus becomes completely dependent on the cell it attacks. Once the virus gains entrance, it manipulates the host cell, running off copies of itself. Now the host cell offers the virus shelter and nourishment. Looking at it from the point of view of the pathogen (the infectious organism), what makes it happy or satisfied is a good meal.

"It takes a membrane," Thomas noted, "to make sense of disorder in biology."[8] The same is true in the physical environment. A river without banks or a lake without borders creates a flood. Clouds, which have no membrane, dissipate into fog or haze.

Anxious, reactive people function in ways similar to a virus attacking a cell. As pathogenic forces invade the body, anxious, reactive people likewise violate the boundaries of others, manipulating them to the reactor's advantage. Viruses and reactive individuals characteristically function in this manner: they respect no boundaries, going where they don't belong, and they must have it their way. They never learn from their experience. Reactive people disguise their self-interest as if it's for the benefit of the whole. Like a virus, they need to escape detection. And they are selective about whom they seek to manipulate.

Pathogens never create infection alone. The host cell's failure always plays a part. The invaded cell gives harbor to the virus, even providing nutrients. Disease processes are enabled. In congregations, boundary violators too often are given a long rope because others refuse to confront the trespassers. When boundaries are inappropriately crossed and people are harmed, no one wants to name the violation. It's as if the disturbance of the group's serenity is a greater offense than the viral-like behavior. Boundary violators go unattended and suffer no consequences. Although going the "second mile" (Matt. 5:41) with offenders is commendable, to go the third, fourth, and fifth mile is indefensible. The lack of attention only enables the repetition of the invasive behavior. Some confuse tolerance with forgiveness and not being confrontive with being loving. The reality, however, is that some individuals are chronically anxious. They lack the capacity to self-regulate. Left unchecked, they continue to harm people. To make human relationships orderly (and civil) requires people with good membranes.

Common Violations

In congregations, typical boundary offenses include one person
or a group of people that

- accuse someone without reasonable cause or without
  initially talking to the accused;
- find "living tissue" in which to grow their rumors or
  careless talk;
- disregard guidelines, policies, and procedures;
- consistently break appointments and miss meetings;
- humiliate people, publicly or privately;
- use verbal pressure to intimidate;
- hold others hostage by threats or demands;
- enlist others to attend secret meetings, distribute peti-
  tions for signature to discredit others, or send unauthorized messages containing disparaging information about
  someone;
- ignore or neglect others, as if they don't exist, for no other
  reason than the others hold different views;
- hide their real agenda by appearing harmless, maybe
  even beneficial: "We're only concerned for the good of
  everybody";
- break an agreement not to talk publicly about a matter
  until a later date;
- withhold affection, approval, and appreciation to demean
  another;
- label others with emotionally-packed words;
- discontinue giving the money they pledged;
- speak on behalf of others, as if they know what the other
  is thinking;
- tell different accounts or share different information,
  depending on the hearers;
- attach fear to any issue in order to control others.

A Story of Broken Borders

Christ Church had no sooner celebrated its 25th anniversary when its pastor, William Conrad, came under suspicion. His friendliness with a widow he was known to be counseling had become the heartbeat of gossip. Confronted by several leaders, the single pastor denied the allegations. A widower himself, he told others that he knew what the woman in question was struggling with and what she needed. But the rumors stuck like glue. His denials were doubted by a couple of leaders who had been his close allies. They hinted that he should resign. A number of other friends adamantly defended him. After five-and-a-half months, Rev. Conrad resigned. But he didn't leave without "breaking some of the furniture," suggesting that some of his staunchest accusers were guilty of the very behavior of which they had attributed to him. Even more devastating, Conrad wrote a letter to the congregation charging them with not supporting their pastors, since he was the third of five forced to leave within the past 18 years.

The leaders took less than a year to find a replacement. Some members thought Conrad could be autocratic at times, acting aloof and unapproachable, yet he worked diligently and had his supporters. Not surprisingly, the congregation selected a successor who was cheerful, outgoing, and more participatory in his leadership style. Pastor Chad Mason appeared to be a welcome relief to many.

What happened next was bizarre. Chad began to make decisions involving funds that were not allocated or approved by the church council. Yet he was not the beneficiary of the financial action. For example, Chad purchased a new, large power mower for the groundskeeper. He gave the athletic director several thousand dollars to purchase new uniforms for several youth and adult teams sponsored by the church; he raised the salary of the associate pastor.

The treasurer who cosigned the checks with the pastor hesitated to mention the purchases, not wanting to upset the congregation again and have another fierce argument over the pastor. He passed a memo to Chad, reminding him that council approval was necessary for expenditures not budgeted and that exceeded a certain amount. But the behavior continued. Pastor Mason used congregational funds to pay the costs for four young people to attend church camp for two weeks, raised the salary of the organist/choir director, and bought hundreds of copies of his friend's new book on prayer and distributed them free of charge.

When the total of these unauthorized expenditures reached $27,000, the treasurer resigned, giving health reasons as the cause. In reality, he was afraid of confronting the pastor and revealing the added costs to the council. He didn't want to be the center of another firestorm. Borrowing terms from the biological model above, he served as "host cell" to Mason's behavior. An interim treasurer completed the remaining four months of the treasurer's term. With the election of a new treasurer, Chad's spending habits were discovered and contested. The former treasurer claimed innocence, explaining he did what the pastor asked him to do. In a meeting with the president of the council and the new treasurer, Chad dismissed the situation, justifying his actions—he received no benefit, the people who received help deserved it, the congregation was profiting since a new mood of satisfaction had emerged, and he hadn't used all the money in his discretionary fund, thus offsetting some of the expenses. Above all, he explained the council was too conservative in its budgeting and needed to stretch its faith. Like many affable and cheerful folks, Chad knew compliments paid dividends. He lavished them on the two church officers, despite their confrontation, but they were not persuaded to back off.

The president contacted an attorney. The treasurer refused to sign checks that were for expenses due to Chad's whims. Nothing deterred Rev. Mason. He exhausted his discretionary funds by paying for a missionary trip for three couples. He forged the treasurer's signature for a bonus check given to the business manager and one to a caterer who had prepared a meal at the church for a meeting of area clergy. The tab was reaching $35,000 in less than one-and-a-half years.

At a church council meeting, the treasurer revealed as many of Mason's self-designated expenditures as he could discover. The president believed, after consulting with a legal advisor, that Rev. Mason could be legally liable. Hearing the report, the council erupted into irrational bouts of anger, resentment, faultfinding, and confusion. Some asked how could something like this continue for 18 months, but others justified Chad's action as being charitable, done without harmful intent. A few threatened to follow the president's ideas about litigation. One member said she was resigning because the council itself was dysfunctional.

Later it was discovered that Chad Mason came from an abusive family. To overcome his insecurity, he learned to give people things or benefits to buy their acceptance. Even though he gained nothing materially, his actions were designed for psychic profit. He eventually left Christ Church and was prosecuted for his behavior, leaving him a debt of about $27,000. Given a second chance elsewhere, Chad liquidated the debt in fewer than four years but, sadly, regressed to similar behavior.

Providing Immunity

Immunity protects against invasion. Leaders supply for the community what the immune system provides for the body. At Christ Church, the new treasurer and the president provided an immune response in dealing with Chad Mason's invasive behavior. To understand how significant immunity is, consider how it works in the body.

Everyone's body is equipped with proof of identity—that is, cells in our body have the same chemical combinations. It's as if they wear identical costumes. Viruses also have a distinct chemical costume. The immune system keeps cells that are bona fide residents separate from illegal aliens. In immunology terminology, the immune system learns to distinguish "self" from "nonself." Once an intruder is spotted, the immune system compares it against the rogues' gallery of known pathogens. If tipped off by resemblances, the immune system arrests and eliminates the intruder. Sorting out self from nonself, the immune system says: "Red blood cells, good guys. Skin cells, part of us. Okay. Virus . . . no good. Toe. Keep."

Biologically, the only way to control a pathogen in the body is through the immune response. Researchers recently discovered two parts to the immune response—the innate and the adaptive. The innate includes "toll-like receptors" that serve as the body's frontline defense against invaders.[9] As gatekeepers who first recognize the presence of a foreign substance, they keep the pathogen in check for a few days, allowing the adaptive system to prepare its defense with the mobilizing of antibodies.

This cellular activity closely parallels what happens in congregations. Usually a few leaders serve as the sentinels, the frontline of defense. They sense something is out of balance or troubling. Without their sensitivity or recognition, the other leaders would not be prepared to act. I have found that these gatekeeper leaders have *proximity*—that is, they are seeing things firsthand or up close. They have *knowledge* about events not widely known. In addition, these leaders realize a significant *cost or consequence* to the congregation could result if something isn't done, and they have a *relationship* with the people who are being harmed. Sometimes these sentinels are not believed. The defenders of Rev. Mason could not accept that someone who did so much good could be a "rogue cell."

Ideally leaders provide an immune response. They discern whether or not something is self or not self, safe or not safe, beneficial or harmful. Is this decision enhancing or retarding our mission? In congregations, as in the human body, we will find intruders. Lacking self-regulation, these individuals may act where they have no authority, say things that have no ground in truth, complain to everyone else except those who can do something about the situation, or place themselves in a position to control the nomination process.

If leaders indeed provide an immune response, what happens when the leadership itself is divided? In both cases—Rev. Conrad (automatic and aloof) and Rev. Mason (a pleaser)—two sides emerged. One group of people saw the functioning of a "foreign substance" or "intruder" and another group saw a "normal" cell. At times this stalemate leads to a healthy struggle around such questions as:

How are we going to function as a community?
What is our defining and unique mission?
What are the norms to which we hold each other accountable?
What are the expectations of each member with regard to
the whole?

Sometimes, however, the leadership's division puts the immune response on hold. If deadlocked for long, involving a third party may be the only course that can break through the impasse.

The "Me Only" Disease

While viruses are foreign substances that invade and manipulate the body's cells for their own purposes, cancer is a disease with its own destructive pattern. A collection of cells that function in ways distinct from normal cells, cancer, too, has parallels with human relationships:

- Unlike normal cells, cancer cells recklessly overproduce. Cancer cells grow. And multiply. Grow and multiply. This is the reason cancer specialists refer to these cells as "immortal" (at least until they kill the cells of which they are a part). Normal cells have a programmed cell death, called

The Forming of a Tumor

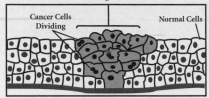

Metastasis

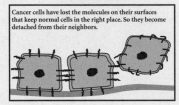

apoptosis, that allows the cells to die and make room for new cells. Cancer cells follow no such commands. They live for themselves.

- Cancer cells lack the mechanism to stick together. They break away to attach themselves to surrounding cells (this process is called *metastasis*). The normal cohesion between cells can be weakened and malignant cells separate from the original mass and travel elsewhere.

- Normal cells eventually differentiate, becoming part of bone and muscle. Cancer cells, however, "de-differentiate." Somehow along the way, the tumor cells lose their capacity to differentiate. Malignant cells do not become part of the mission of the living tissue. They say to the rest of the organism, "We have no need of you. We are the center of the universe. Your job is to feed us." As with so many immature individuals, what they do is uncoordinated with the needs or constraints of their neighbors. Having no regard for the rest of the body, these disloyal cells live for themselves, pursuing their own interests in conflict with the host.[10]

Dealing with people who function in a "Me Only" manner is time-consuming and energy-draining. They are determined to have it their way, regardless. They are so perverse that cultivating relationships or engaging them in reasoned discourse is nearly impossible. And in congregations that have a tendency to resolve all troubles neatly and to pull back from ambiguous situations, leaders are tempted to leave these people alone rather than establish appropriate boundaries. Instead of providing immunity for the congregation, they offer cover for the people who lack self-regulation.

A Personal Note

As with any human organization, congregations need oversight. Administration is a service, a ministry, as the word itself indicates. Leaders are servants in a community. Shaping and preserving boundaries is an essential service of congregational leaders. Theologian Larry Rasmussen astutely asserts:

> Governance is a crucial part of our life together for at least two reasons. One reason is simple: life is a mess. It is not *only* a mess, but it is a mess. Some of it is a mess all the time, all of it is a mess some of the time, and disordered houses do not stand. Just as our bodies do poorly without food, bodies politic do poorly without governance. Communities, in order to be communities, must be ordered, cared for, led. The other reason is equally noted: governance is necessary for the positive flourishing of life.[11]

Applying Rasmussen's comments to this chapter's microbiology model, I would add that, just as bodies need immunity to be healthy, bodies politic do poorly without immunity. People in our communities who lack the ability to regulate self will invade, intrude, trespass, attack, and rudely interfere—making a mess of things. Silence and avoidance on the part of the leader only enable the "disease" process.

One of the nagging questions facing leaders is how long can the mess be endured before it becomes a major infection. Love, after all, is long-suffering. Indeed it is. But love is not long-suffering and foolish. Love is not overindulgent. Love is not a failure of nerve. Love suffers long so that something new can be erected out of the old. Yet love does not suffer long because it is anxious about naming and confronting the violation. Love doesn't put up with harmful boundary intrusion, because it would agitate the community's peace. Long-suffering love is about doing away with suffering that issues from the harm of others, not being an accomplice to the harmful invasion.

The Leader's Notebook

Boundaries in Emotional Systems

- Beginning with cells, all living things have boundaries.
- As a living thing, a person needs to develop and sustain a "cell wall."
- With a healthy boundary in place, a person knows where she begins and ends.
- Ideally, a person's boundary (cell wall) will be solid enough so he thinks, feels, and acts for "self," yet flexible enough to maintain connection with others.
- A person's boundary defines her territory and protects her space from invasion by others.
- Having good boundaries, a person focuses on his own functioning, being careful not to violate the boundaries of others.

- In emotional systems, less mature people lacking self-regulation can become invasive and unregulated.
- Leaders must encourage boundary respect.
- By providing immunity, leaders enforce boundaries to the benefit of the whole.
- With healthy boundaries, love is possible.

PART 3

THE LEADER'S CHALLENGES

For congregational leaders the time for testing will come, as will the occasion for elevating spirits and celebrating. The low periods are painful. Your energy is exhausted and your spirit is drained. For good reason, the apostle Paul urged the early Christians not to grow weary in well doing for in due season they would reap (Gal. 6:7–10). In anxious times, congregations are especially in need of their leaders' wisdom, integrity, patience, and faithfulness. The highs are natural periods for rejuvenation, thanksgiving, and sharing joy—activities for building up the congregation's positive "emotional bank account."

Your challenge is twofold. You will sometimes be asked to deal with sorrow, anger, anxiety, even evil. What will you do when reactivity erupts and tranquility is shattered? Second, you will want to contribute to the congregation's positive emotional and spiritual well being. How can you ensure an increase of spiritual growth and goodwill?

For you, the leader, there are no off-seasons, because every season under the sun requires leadership. All seasons are important, but none more so than the strong season when emotions run high.

Chapter 7

We versus They

In this chapter we will study the nature and outcomes of conflict in congregations.

The church has been far too fearful of conflict. Congregational leaders need to come to a new position, one that regards conflict as inevitable, possibly essential. Conflict is a part of living. Too often, however, we react in a primitive way that merely results in a "we versus they" scenario. How we regard conflict is a test and an act of leadership. How can we turn trouble into opportunity? Most critically, when conflict arises, how can it be seen as a learning point for change and an experience that can strengthen the congregation's functioning? Not all conflicts are equal. Some are harsh and bitter. Yet many conflicts can contribute to the growth of a congregation and make a positive contribution. The quality of leadership applied to the situation determines the outcome.

embrace conflict

The Gathering Storm

Church conflict is a growth industry. My experience tells me that about four out of ten congregations in any five-year period face a moderate to serious conflict. About one third of them take effective steps to recognize and address the situation. Not only are the number of incidences rising, but also the number of people who are stubborn, deceptive, and mean. Commenting about society in general, film critic Adam Gopnik claims that there is a growing "kind of weird, free-form nastiness—spleen without purpose."[1] Against the background of the church as a loving, welcoming community, the nastiness is clearly out of place. "When you stir in conviction with anger," former priest Garret Keizer observes, "the anger is brighter, louder, and more willful. Add rage and the anger is wild."[2]

If conflict is intense and protracted, the battles drain the congregation's energy and resources. Meanwhile those embroiled in the bitter rifts demand super simple and immediate solutions—anything to ease their discomfort. Most people seek a quick return to normalcy. But the mere reduction of anxiety is fool's gold. The lessening of tensions is mistaken for the resolution of the conflict. Restoration of equilibrium is not a sign that the congregation's functioning is improved. Certainly pain has receded. But congregation leaders need to ask themselves, did the pain become a teacher? Did it provoke any new awareness? Did clarity develop to inform decision making? Were necessary changes implemented? If nothing is learned, if nothing changes, if important action is not taken, if new safeguards are not set in place, and if a sense of mission is not revived, the battle will return, maybe with different people over different issues but not with different functioning. Essentially, the suffering will have yielded no benefit.

Conflict Habits

At almost any level (national, judicatory, local), little is being done to increase understanding of congregational strife, much less to improve the management of it or to prevent it. Effective responses on the part of the congregation are slow to develop. A high percentage of congregations are not prepared to face the animosity, to take action to address the problem, and to be sufficiently patient to heal. Rather, congregations develop patterns of survival behavior. When trouble brews, they rely on the conflict habits listed below, none of which are remotely helpful: peace mongering, false attribution, neglect and other forms of denial, such as avoidance or accommodation and idealistic expectations.

Peace Mongering

Peace mongering is common. With tranquility and stability reigning as premium values, congregational leaders adapt to their most recalcitrant and immature people, allowing them to use threats and tantrums as levers of influence. Malcontents' complaints never seem to cease. Unwilling to confront the constant critic, leaders set the table for the unhappy souls to have a movable feast of anxiety. By appeasing rather than opposing, leaders give control to reactive forces. Feed them once and leaders can be sure they will be back for more.

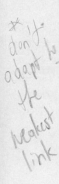

False Attribution

Another habit, mostly attributable to clergy, is their equation of conflict with sin or evil. If a fracture deepens in the congregation, they name the primary suspect: "This is the work of Satan." In a congregation I served as a consultant, a pastor said that if only people would tell him how he sinned against them, he could ask for their forgiveness. A leader in the congregation finally told him that incompetence is a fact, not a sin. Sometimes the primary issues in a conflict have nothing to do with transgression or darkness. Simply, there are fundamental differences or inadequacies, and a change is needed for people to flourish.

Neglect or Denial

Leaders at times opt for sheer neglect or denial to alleviate emotional discomfort, as if inattention could disable incredibly strong forces. Instead of giving in, leaders ignore. But a conflict suppressed only needs a new stroke of anxiety to excite reactivity once again. Anxiety deferred is not the same as anxiety managed.

Avoidance or Accommodation

These two behaviors, also forms of denial, tend to be more typical of clergy than of lay leaders, which complicates efforts to confront congregational conflict. According to several studies, clergy are neither well prepared for handling conflict nor willing to engage it. Generally, clergy are highly motivated to give and receive affection. Their warmth and kindness contribute to their pastoral qualities. But these same qualities limit their capacity for proactive behavior: being decisive and taking positions. Clergy hesitate to be assertive because such behavior may be seen as endangering the congregation's harmony and stoking the fires of unrest.

In conflict management analyses, clergy score high in *avoidance, accommodation,* and *compromise.* Clergy score quite low compared to the general population in preference for *assertiveness* and *collaboration,* more proactive styles to engage conflict. The image of clergy as "The Right Reverend Friendly" has not changed significantly.

Idealistic Expectations

Congregations continue to impose an idealized image upon themselves. The expectation of many church members is that the church will always reflect and demonstrate love. They think that acknowledging divisions or separations admits to a defect. Not only is the congregation to be the epitome of love but also a replica of a fantasy: warmth and closeness are always found here. If intimacy is threatened, people will hide their disagreements, conceal their disappointments, and place a taboo on certain emotions. No wonder conflict is denied and church members receive little experience in dealing with problems of willfulness, sabotage, immature behavior, and raw emotionality. Too often someone will cite Acts 2 as the portrayal of an ideal congregation:

> All who believed were together and had all things in common; they would sell their possessions and goods and distribute the proceeds to all, as any had need. Day by day, as they spent much time together in the temple, they broke bread at home and ate their food with glad and generous hearts, praising God and having the goodwill of all the people. And day by day the Lord added to their number those who were being saved.
>
> —Acts 2:44–47

They forget this is a momentary picture of life in the early church. When we read further in the book of Acts, we discover that the euphoria gives way to lying and pretenses (Acts 5, Ananias and Sapphira deceive their community); serious ruptures between two culturally distinct groups (Acts 6, the Hellenists murmur against the Jews); theological contention (Acts 15:5–11, the community debates whether circumcision was required of Gentiles); and disagreement (Acts 15:36–39, Paul and Barnabas part company). The Acts 2 snapshot may be the ideal, but most congregational living is much less than ideal and reflects the range seen in the entire book of Acts.

With the expansion of Christianity, the apostle Paul acknowledges disputes and admonishes contentious people:

- "I fear that there may perhaps be quarreling, jealousy, anger, selfishness, slander, gossip, conceit, and disorder" (2 Cor. 12:20).
- "If . . . you bite and devour one another, take care that you are not consumed by one another" (Gal. 5:15).
- "Put away from you all bitterness and wrath and anger and wrangling and slander, together with all malice" (Eph. 4:31).

The apostle recognizes the knotty realities groups face when diverse people from every race, income bracket, temperament, age level, philosophical persuasion, or family background come together. "When church folk feel like their world view or personal integrity is being questioned or condemned," Professor Hugh Halverstadt claims, "they often become emotionally violent or violating. Any means are used to justify the goal of emotional self-protection."[3]

The New Aggressiveness

Besides exhibiting these conflict habits, congregations are experiencing an increase in belligerent actions. The following conflict scenario is repeated regularly: friction between two parties intensifies; a series of painful exchanges follow; the sides deadlock; finally someone or some group requests or demands a person's removal or they threaten to remove themselves. Any removal would bring relief to some but fuel resentment among others. Instead of being conciliatory or engaging in problem solving, people become polarized. Edwin Friedman in *Generation to Generation* remarks:

> What creates polarization is not the actual content of the issue on which a family "splits." It is rather emotional processes that foster conflict of wills (efforts to convert one another). To

this plays out in families, workplaces, & political arena.

leader must resist simply reaching to the reactivity of others

the extent a leader can contain his or her reactiveness to the reactivity of followers, primarily by focusing on self functioning rather than by trying to change the functioning of others, intensity tends to wane, and polarization or a cutoff that, like a tango, always takes two, is less likely to be the result.[4]

A congregation's balance is disturbed more by people's strong reaction to one another than by reaction to the issue or the event itself. Unfortunately, today's polarization is maintained by a bold competitiveness. The goal of conflict is to win. No thought is given to "we sink or swim together." Instead, one party swims and the other must sink. The more aggressive behavior becomes, the more the objective shifts from wanting to win toward wanting to hurt. In congregations the aggression is seldom physical; it is more often psychological, such as belittling and shaming the other party. Conflict is no longer a time for learning but for conquering. Domination supplants education. Civility and courtesy give way to sneers and shouting. Heat, not light, is the outcome. Forgiveness and reconciliation may not even be mentioned or considered. Author Garret Keizer notes, "One of the things we fear most is losing a battle. It is as if the primal emotion of anger arises in us because every conflict in some way recalls some primal conflict, when our very lives were a stake."[5]

When a conflict regresses to a forceful competition, we are apt to see the following:

Yes! skewed sense of victory

this happens at my house

- People function at the level of the primitive brain, breaking everything into this or that, black or white, plus or minus. The primitive instinct neatly narrows complexity into "we versus they." In fact, some people gain support for their "side" by deepening the polarization, even promising to maintain it.

Yes!

- Worse yet, when emotional juices are sprayed on the issues, fervor and passion knock reason out of the picture.

emotion vs. reason

The original differences themselves are no longer sustaining the differing. Emotionality drives the competition. When that happens, people will not respond to reasonableness, insight, or love. With the yes-or-no thinking dividing the house, the objective all comes down to winning. Bring down the enemy!

- Behaviors become more aggressive—shouting down the opposite side, belittling them, using in-your-face tactics to intimidate, threatening legal action against someone, stacking the deck with supporters.
- Lying increases, taking many forms—half truths, withholding information, inflating statistics and bloating claims, fabricating events, releasing publicly that was to be private, double talk, and false attributions.
- Self-righteousness emerges. One party thinks she can use any means to achieve her end because her cause is "right." No one plays by the rules now. A person takes any advantage he can, even introducing God as his ally.

"Being right is not too difficult. You choose your perception, you select your information. You leave out what does not suit you, you drag in some general-purpose value words, you throw in a sneer or two about the opposition, and you are a fine fellow who has made fine speech."

—Edward de Bono[6]

Different Outcomes

A conflict-free congregation is incongruent not only with reality but even more with biblical theology. Jesus upset many people emotionally. The life of Jesus takes place against a backdrop of suspicion, opposition, and crucifixion. The Christian story is underlined with conflict. Early on, we encounter the *emotional reactivity* of the religious leaders, who see Jesus as a threat to their authority and belief system. Eventually the tension between the roaming preacher and the established religious order comes to a dramatic point. Tension leads to crucifixion.

The church has had divisions from its inception. No doubt, it has fought senseless battles, squandered its resources on frivolous issues, sent negative signals to society, shattered its unity, and forfeited chances to share its goodwill. Some churches work through the reactive period and emerge stronger. Others shuffle from crisis to crisis. What makes the difference in outcomes?

Nowhere in the Bible is tranquility preferred to truth or harmony to justice. Certainly reconciliation is the goal of the gospel, yet seldom is reconciliation an immediate result. If people believe the Holy Spirit is directing the congregation into the truth, wouldn't this alone encourage Christians who have differing notions to grapple with issues respectfully, lovingly, and responsively? If potent issues are avoided because they might divide the community, what type of witness is the congregation to the pursuit of truth?

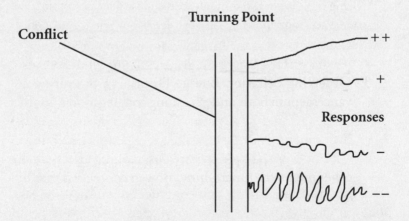

Figure 7.1
There comes a turning point when the conflict either creates positive responses (+) or degenerates into a negative affair (-).

The turning point comes when the conflict either creates positive responses or degenerates into a negative affair. The positive path is aided by these actions:

1. Respecting the sheer strength of survival instincts. The will to survive is extremely strong. Brains are constructed to react to threat, not contemplate it. In the presence of high tension, expect behavior to be substandard for a while. Being patient in order to move toward improvement, the leader will not make choices driven by the anxiety of the moment. Thoughtfulness will reappear as the primitive instincts subside. First, however, the craziness has to play itself out: blaming, misinforming, taking defensive action, shouting impassioned comments, repeating unfounded rumors, exaggerating events, and relying on worse-case consequences.

2. Seeking clarity. With misinformation, rumor, and exaggeration bouncing off the wall, confusion is always in attendance. Ask questions. Weigh whether information is reliable and congruent. But also remember that clarity won't always be comfortable for everyone. Some people will wear emotional blinders. Stay on course. Ultimately, people prefer hearing the truth rather than distortion.

3. Observing behavior. Bowen Theory is a promising advancement in both understanding congregational conflict and regulating its noxious effects. The theory describes the human family as a natural, living, multigenerational system in which each person's functioning affects all the other members' functioning. Bowen contended that human systems function in ways similar to other life forms. What distinguishes the human family from the rest of nature is the human capacity to observe automatic behavior and substitute principles for impulses in managing it. By developing more thoughtful approaches to life's changes

and challenges, we can behave with a wider repertoire of responses and choose from a spectrum of choices.

As I discussed in part 1, Bowen used the terms *emotional* and *emotionality* to signify behavior that is impulsive, instinctual. Remember the lizard. Emotionality is wired into our protoplasm for rapid, defensive purposes and is necessary for us to confront threats and to survive. Emotional processes are driven by automatic behaviors. Sometimes, instead of acting rationally, we flare up in anger or pull back in fear. At other times, we maintain our composure and retain our ability to think things through.

Imagine a member in the congregation who is a habitual complainer. No matter what the condition, issue, or topic, the member finds something wrong. But the complainer is only half of the equation. In order for the carping censure to continue, others must reinforce it. Sometimes this happens by adding fuel to the fire, counterattacking the attacker. Sometimes the behavior is maintained, because others cut themselves off from the critic. But distancing merely raises the stakes for the unhappy soul, and the complaints become deeper or more frequent. For any conflict to continue and to get out of control, a generator of anxiety and an amplifier are needed. They feed each other.

4. Informing. In the early stages of a conflict, it is almost impossible to over-inform. As much information as possible is needed. Providing information tends to minimize the need for people to create information for themselves through gossip and embellishments of what they have heard from rumor. By communicating forthrightly, leaders also treat the members as mature adults who can handle whatever information is shared, not as children who need to be protected from bad news.

5. Working with the healthy individuals. To move beyond people's survival instincts, leaders will be more successful when they work with the most mature, motivated people in the congregation. No one can pour insight into unmotivated people. These individuals may be on both sides of the conflict.

6. Structuring a process. An anxiety-infected system spreads anxiety in all directions. People increasingly become confused, angry, and disgusted, and inch toward near-despair. The flow of anxiety needs to be contained, and nothing does this better than placing a structure over the anxiety-ridden field. When people sense that there will be an orderly effort in place, people think things are not totally out of control. People yearn for clear and decisive action. When specific goals are followed, the people have confidence that the congregation has the means to get out of the misery they have gotten into and to move forward again. Good structure corrals anxiety.

7. Reframing the situation. Instead of anxiously bemoaning what's happening, leaders can frame the situation as an opportunity for growth. Through this painful encounter, the congregation will emerge stronger, knowing better ways to live together.

8. Building up the congregation's positive emotional bank account. Once a conflict subsides, leaders provide after-care, which could embrace many options. John Gottman, the marriage researcher mentioned in chapter 3, suggests one. He believes marriage counselors spend too much time helping couples to fight fair or to learn how to handle their partner better. Gottman suggests that counselors should spend more time helping marriage partners promote a steady flow of positive interactions in their relationship, which, according to longitudinal studies, is a critical ingredient of long and rewarding

marriages. Building up a robust emotional bank account of goodwill, fun, care, and respect serves marriage more than reducing fighting. Moreover, the account draws interest.

Congregations, too, can benefit from their steady flow of positive programs, ministerial acts, and supportive gatherings. When tensions threaten relationships, people can draw from their positive emotional investments as a resource to move past the pressing moment. People know that the congregation, even if in tension, is a place of warmth, care, and benefits. The joy and rewards of positive relationships promote motivation for breaking the impasse and not permitting the conflict to become brutal competition.

9. Bringing in a third party. Some conflict becomes so convoluted and emotional that those affected become entrenched in their "our side" bias. The parties involved in a dispute are too closely involved to get a wider view. To dislodge the ensuing impasse, an outside third party with a more objective set of eyes is needed. Select someone outside of the emotional system who will be fair and frank. The people involved in the dispute are too close to what is happening to get an overview or to get a sense of perspective. It is also difficult for them to carry out the thinking operations necessary to bring clarity to a situation when emotional factors run strong. People construct a coherent argument to support their viewpoint rather than to explore other points of view.[7]

A Personal Note

In conflict, both parties begin with full confidence in the strength of their case. Soon they realize that neither side is likely to gain an easy victory. Now it is a matter of "hanging in there," hoping the other side will give up.

Bogged down in a standoff, people are apt to use conflict as a way of carrying out a competition, rather than as an education. The situation becomes increasingly negative and hostile. People are anxious about "losing" or appearing "weak" or being humiliated. This only stiffens their will to prevail.

Though not easily accomplished, what is required is action, not victory. Someone has to provide a way to focus and to engage the people's imaginative capacities. How can we move from argument to explanation? If we don't, we're entangled in nothing but a trial of strength. How can we use our ingenuity to address our predicament instead of defeating the other side? Leaders are needed who can help design an outcome instead of arbitrating or refereeing an emotional wrestling match.

The Leader's Notebook

Twenty Observations

I have worked with troubled churches for 20 years. I never cease to learn from these experiences. The list below includes some of what I have learned about congregations in times of conflict.

1. Most people are interested in relieving their own anxiety rather than managing the crisis or planning for a clear direction. Their primary goal is anxiety reduction not congregational renewal.
2. Under certain conditions, anxiety is neutral. As much as possible, effective leaders normalize anxiety. Considering what is happening, anxiety's presence is what we would expect. By normalizing, people will not automatically think it is because the community is flawed.

3. If anxiety is high, people lose their capacity to be self-reflective. They look outward, not at themselves. Self-awareness is dim. And the ability to identify with the life processes of others is impaired.

4. Peace is often preferred over justice. Congregational members can resist or be hesitant about taking stands, making decisions, or charting a course of action that would offend or upset the community. By placing a premium on togetherness, they play into the hands of the most dependent people who can threaten to incite disharmony as a way to receive what they want. When such superficial harmony—so-called peace—must prevail, then the pursuit of justice often is sacrificed and others who are involved become excused from responsibility.

5. If an individual becomes the lightening rod for people's anxiety and cannot extricate him- or herself from that position through self-differentiation (or the environment is so perverse that no one can escape from that position), trying to maintain his or her position or presence in the emotional system is unproductive and as well as painful.

6. All disease processes are enabled. Viruses need host cells. Not all people designated by anxious systems as the patient are sick. The illness is in the interactive system, to which the following observations attest:

   "All neuroses have accomplices" (Carl Jung).

   Anxiety not resolved in one relationship will be acted out in another relationship.

   "Unless the leader has a degree of self-knowledge and self-understanding, there is the risk that he or she may use the organization to address his or her own neuroses" (Peter Senge et al).[8]

7. The way we use information is an emotional phenomenon; what we hear and don't hear, what we
   remember, how we gather and exclude data are
   all connected to emotional processes. We gravi-
   tate toward information that coincides with our
   viewpoints and that promises to contribute to our
   survival.

[handwritten margin note: we hear what we want to hear]

8. The healing process for midrange to severely anxious
   congregations takes two to five years.

9. Losses (membership, offerings, attendance) will
   result no matter what choices are made. Most congregations regain their losses within two years.

10. Secrets—that is, hidden agendas and invisible loy-
    alties—in most cases need to be brought to light.
    What about sin and evil? Expect it; expose it. To
    expose the demonic, name it (recall the story of
    Jesus and the demoniac in Mark 5).

11. Reactivity can issue from people who are leaders,
    erudite, talented, wealthy, well-educated, pious,
    charming, or normally calm folks. None of the
    above characteristics indicate that these individuals
    are mature emotionally.

[handwritten margin note: anyone can be reactive]

12. Issues must be clearly identified and individuals
    must be challenged to act. No anxious congregation
    can handle more than three to five issues at a time.
    The issues must be condensed.

13. The sabotage of a process to deal with conflict
    should be expected. The usual saboteurs will be
    those who are losing control or not getting what
    they want from the process.

14. Murray Bowen claimed that all dyads are unstable.
    Therefore the basic molecule of all relationship sys-
    tems is a triangle (the use of a third party to reduce
    tension between a twosome). A Swahili proverb

reads: "When the elephants fight, it's the grass that gets crushed." Triangle formation is natural. Triangulation is another matter. It happens when the third party allows the original dyad to escape responsibility for its actions by assuming their anxiety and taking responsibility for them. Whenever a congregation brings in a third party, such as an intervention team, there is a triangle. Triangulation would occur if the team became anxious and felt responsible for the conflict's outcome.

15. Five styles of managing conflict have become commonplace: accommodating, problem solving, compromising, avoiding, and fighting. They are useful for recognizing general patterns of behavior under pressure. But they are not helpful when used as predictors—"Oh, Susan never takes a stand. She'll compromise on anything." People like Susan do not function in the same way in every context. At home Susan may compromise but at work she's quite a problem solver. Even in the same conflict, people may shift from one style to another. One may begin as a fighter, only with time to become an accommodator. Further, not all avoiders or problem solvers are equal. There's a range to their functioning. People's functioning is not determined by a style but by the context.

16. Recent research challenges the prevailing assumptions about conflict behavior being mutually exclusive. For example, direct fighting and problem solving are more effective in combination than they are in isolation. The continuous repetition of fighting, then problem solving, and then fighting is effective.

17. How the conflict is framed affects the behavior of those involved. When the conflict is conceptual-

beware of assumptions about people's behavior

ized as cost or benefit, the participants' behavior changes. People become more involved if they anticipate losses as a result of the conflict than if they anticipate gains. Losses arouse greater emotional force. Researchers found that a prospect of loss led to less yielding behavior. Even when the opponent is about to suffer a loss, there is more cooperation from the other side than if the opponent enjoyed a profit.[9]

18. No emotional system will change unless the members of the system change how they interact with one another. Patterns of behavior tend toward rigidity. Conflict may be necessary to jolt and jar the shape of things in order to reshape the pattern. But the degree to which that change is positive or negative depends on the leadership present to respond to it.

19. The parties involved in a rift are in a poor position to settle the dispute if anxiety is high and rampant. Being too closely and emotionally involved in a circumstance, they will find it difficult to provide a fair overview.

20. Final or perfect solutions are not available. Conflict leaves things messy. The best solutions to insolvable problems are the approximate solutions—ones that prepare a system for new learning and a new beginning.

Chapter 8

Rocking the Emotional Boat

In this chapter we will examine what happens when the leader decides to challenge the congregation's balance.

The last people we would expect to create a general disturbance are the congregational leaders themselves. However, a time may come when you, the leader, will have to challenge the congregation, upsetting its balance. You may have to disturb the calm with distressing news, take action that will not prove popular, and make decisions that will ignite an emotional uproar. Such a time will require courage, "the courage," Old Testament scholar Walter Brueggeman suggests, "to be fully present in insistent, asserting ways, the kind of courage that finest Christian piety often avoids."[1]

Emotional systems seek balance and stability. The technical term for this coherence is *homeostasis* (stay the same). In the human body, temperature, salt levels, and blood sugar levels are subject to homeostatic forces. When these levels drop or rise, the body automatically seeks to rebalance them. Congregations, as a system, also seek to maintain balance and stability even if their leaders are working to establish more effective patterns of interaction.

So as Not to Upset Anyone

The Indo-European word *leith,* for leader, means "to go forth, to die." In the Dutch language, one of the words for leader might be translated "martyr"—one who suffers. Is it foolish to ask, "How can I lead and stay alive"? Perhaps not. I have seen capable, honest leaders depicted as inept and devious; I have seen leaders of great integrity castigated for being selfishly motivated, and ultimately turned away. Under pressure, people demand answers and assurances. Their expectation is that leaders will bring stability, provide safety, and offer quick solutions. Alongside these expectations, people believe that leaders will do all this with a minimum of disruption and no surprises. If not, resistance is inevitable. You, the leader, will be rebuked. You will be accused of exaggerating the situation. You will be rejected for a myriad of reasons—for being a bully, a "softie," political, power hungry, blind and obtuse, dysfunctional. For sure, someone will ask for disciplinary measures or a vote of confidence. Resistance, leaders must remember, is part of the leadership process. Too many leaders retreat or capitulate when resistance becomes loud, rude, and messy, because the unspoken rule is "so as not to upset anyone." Leaders become pleasers. In return for the pleasing, they escape hostilities. Harvard professor of government Ronald Heifetz states, "Followers want comfort, stability, and solutions from their leaders, but that's babysitting. Real leaders ask hard questions and knock people out of their comfort zones. Then they manage the resulting distress."[2]

Humans have a strong tendency to group together and commune. Once this happens, they become comfortable together. They find a sense of satisfaction in standing shoulder-to-shoulder and heart-to heart. All this comes naturally and is a function of the midbrain, the part of the brain where bonding is processed. It is difficult for individuals who have a close bond to step back, look around, and see things objectively. Not willing to be unpopular with the group, leaders let themselves be co-opted by emotional pressure from the gathering. Enjoying the familiarity the group provides, people just don't like novelty. Systems resist being upset.

Brave Souls

Leaders will see things that are disturbing, abnormal, and possibly corrupt. Usually, only those who are up close see these behaviors or circumstances. The vast majority of people have no knowledge or experience with the troubling matter. They see the positive and the good. Even if leaders confront the problem quietly and respectfully, however, sooner or later the critical situation becomes public. The leader is now at the hub of the storm. Consider the situation at Seaside Church where leaders put themselves on the line:

At Seaside Church, what could have been better? Glance at these glowing features:

- The congregation has completed a $12-million building program.
- More than 200 new members have put Seaside at the 2,000 threshold and have increased its average Sunday worship attendance to 850.
- Many of the new members are under age 45, bringing energy and fresh perspectives to the church.
- A full staff of 12 is in place, and the recent loss of a respected associate pastor who, it was rumored, could not work with the senior pastor, is receding in people's minds.
- The governing board is an assortment of capable lay people.

- The senior pastor is highly touted for his preaching and teaching, for being a very spiritual person, and for developing a strong men's ministry.
- Pledges and offerings are not increasing significantly but are at least holding their own against expenses.

This calm surface began to crack. First, word was spreading in church groups that friction existed between the senior pastor, Rev. Whitney Brown, and several members of the board. Supposedly, a number of staff members had complained about Whitney Brown's capricious behavior to the board's personnel committee. The head of the ministry with seniors, they reported, had resigned to pursue other interests. Whitney reported to the board that the termination was voluntary, when, in fact, the senior pastor had insisted on his resignation. At the same time, the other associate pastor revealed to a few board members that Whitney had also misinformed them regarding the departure of the respected associate mentioned above.

The board pressed these issues with Whitney, but he downplayed their significance and "corrected" the misunderstandings. When he was asked if he had given three staff members salary raises (those known to be staunch supporters) but blocked raises for other staff members, Whitney simply responded that he was fair to all and used good judgment. Yet another board member asked if Whitney had altered an evaluation of a staff member he didn't like, making the evaluation quite negative, contrary to what the supervisor had originally written. Whitney admitted he checked all evaluations and would make his own notations, but he did not acknowledge any negative modifications. Several board members suggested that he be relieved of any staff oversight and become primarily the congregation's spiritual leader.

The issues became even more complicated in the next several months. Whitney's defensiveness, evasions, and dissembling stirred up suspicion and opposition. Reed Price, a solid supporter of Whitney Brown and a board member, arranged a private meeting with the senior pastor. Reed spoke appreciatively of Whitney. But Whitney mistook his initial appreciation as unquestionable support. "I can always count on you, Reed," Whitney boasted. "You are a godly man." Reed, however, had come to confront Whitney about his lack of truthfulness and pitting staff members against one another. Though he expressed appreciation for his comments, Reed told Whitney he no longer trusted him and thought that he needed clinical help. Whitney reacted with shock: "I'm appalled that you would believe the falsehoods and attacks." He told Reed that his spiritual life was weak and Satan had snared his soul. Nonetheless, Whitney promised to pray for Reed so that he might be restored to the "spiritual tower of strength" he used to be. Reed heard his comments as hollow and insecure posturing. These were the perfunctory remarks, Reed thought, of a spiritual imposter. "Whitney," he responded, "you are manipulating me as you do your staff."

Reed left with ambivalence. How could there be this mixture of good and bad—Whitney Brown's biblical sermons and his outlandish lying, the uplifting words and the mistreatment of people? Reed's head and heart were not at peace with one another. Originally Whitney's supporter, Reed became Whitney's truth teller. "My integrity," he told me later, "was the key." He personally liked Whitney, felt incredibly indebted to him for being present when Reed was in need, and respected his spiritual insights. "I had nothing against him. No revenge, no hate," Reed continued, "no rivalry, no hateful feelings. I felt no need to attack him."

Reed mentioned that he finally came to see that Whitney was not the same person publicly as he was privately. "I couldn't stand silently aside and allow him to humiliate and harm people like that." Ironically, Reed reminded himself that he learned about blasphemy from Whitney Brown. "A brood of vipers" and "bones of the dead" are two allusions Matthew's Gospel uses to identify profane leaders in Jesus's day (3:7; 23:27). "Jesus reserved some of his sharpest words," Reed stated, "for deceivers."

In the meantime, Whitney called and rallied his supporters. A good number of them came from the newer members. Their advice to Whitney was not always the wisest, because a congregation's ethos is often at odds with the ethos typical of other communities. Tactics acceptable in other domains, especially threats to employ legal muscle, are often rejected in congregational life. A couple of his supporters attempted to intimidate Reed with legal action, however.

The majority of the people were out of the loop. They were quite stunned to read about the problem in the newsletter and quite frustrated to learn only a few details. But the two sides formed rapidly, one side viewing Whitney's problems as managerial and the other side as clinical. The pro-Whitney forces campaigned to have him take a few managerial courses or to relieve him of administrative duties. "Let's not forfeit his great spiritual influence," one strong advocate remarked, "for a little remedial management work." Reed Price and other board members countered that Whitney's difficulties were more personal than technical.

With emotionality swelling, sharp attacks against the governing board increased. People threatened to remove the board from office, belittled their judgments, and questioned their motives. A small but vocal group assembled information to disparage individuals on the board, charging them with being out to get Whitney because they themselves had been ousted or fired in their own jobs (though no one ever corroborated these claims). It was simply an old ploy: "Let's save Whitney by destroying Reed."

The board held its ground. They stayed the course by drawing upon their own emotional stamina, operating on clear principles, and encouraging one another. One of the leaders said to me: "It was the perfect storm in that the right people came together at the right time and saw the same things, and they couldn't conceal it."

Eventually Whitney Brown resigned. Followed by several hundred emotionally devoted followers, he became pastor of a new, independent congregation. Whitney and his new leadership team (called "spiritual advisors") developed a covenant for membership in which all members vowed to be obedient to the spiritual direction of the senior pastor. Manipulation, we can see, knows no limits. Seaside recovered but with a smaller membership and reduced staff, perhaps a few years away from matching the same levels before the division occurred.

One additional detail is noteworthy in Seaside's story. Prior to Reed Price's private conversation with Whitney, at least seven other leaders had addressed similar issues with him in private meetings over the six-year span of Whitney Brown's tenure as pastor. Either not receiving a response or hearing "Don't you worry," these leaders left the congregation in frustration.

Solo opposition is easily ignored or squelched. At Seaside a sufficient number of leaders, respected and known to be fair and thoughtful people, presented the problem. Enough members in the congregation knew these individuals were not vindictive or rash reactionaries, therefore their position warranted attention. Moreover, these leaders didn't return reactivity with reactivity. Their grace under pressure attracted a hearing from other mature people. Perhaps most of all, they did not see their responsibility as one of preserving harmony at the expense of their integrity or the abuse of others. They rocked the emotional system at Seaside by naming a problem and stunning the members. They knew there would be casualties because even some of them had been avid admirers of Whitney Brown.

Technical or Adaptive Problems

In addressing Rev. Whitney Brown's leadership, Seaside's members had come down on one of two sides—Whitney's managerial skills needed attention or his personal qualities were the heart of the problem. In their book *Leadership on the Line: Staying*

Alive through the Dangers of Leading, Ronald Heifetz and Martin Linsky, professors at Harvard University, distinguish between what they call *technical* and *adaptive* problems. Each problem requires a different response. Confusing the two types of problems will result in ineffective responses. When we are dealing with technical problems, we use know-how and follow a set of procedures. Adaptive problems, however, involve challenges to deeply held values and well-entrenched attitudes. They require new learning.[3]

Technical Problems

- Problems are amenable to solutions.
- People already know what to do and how to do it.
- Leaders know the answer and take corrective action.
- Problems are not trivial, but solutions are within a person's abilities.
- Solutions are not necessarily easy, but expertise and knowledge are available.

Adaptive Problems

- Problems demand change in values, attitudes, and behaviors.
- People's hearts and minds need to change, not only their likes and dislikes.
- Problems surface that no existing technical expertise can solve.
- Leaders ask questions that challenge people's beliefs.
- Problems require a mindset shift that will result in some loss, especially for people who benefited from previous circumstances or patterns.
- People are challenged to use their competence to bring about new solutions. Leaders bring people's attention to the problem and expect them to take responsibility for it.
- Problem solving involves new experiments, uncertainty, and loss.

technical

The members of Seaside Congregation had to treat the problem of Whitney Brown's behavior. The managerial proponents had a technical view: "The presenting problem is clear and there's a fix for it." Members wanted to send Whitney to a few management workshops, thinking that would solve the problem. Some others also regarded the problem as a technical one, suggesting Whitney be relieved of all management responsibilities and become the preaching, teaching, and visioning pastor. Others proposed another technical solution by asking the unhappy staff members to leave and the frustrated leaders to resign. All of these solutions are familiar ways to handle problems.

adaptive

A core of congregation leaders, however, sought adaptive solutions, believing the situation demanded more than a few cosmetics: "It's clinical. Behavioral changes are necessary. New learning has to take place." In reality, they were asking Whitney Brown to do what they themselves had done. They had to adapt. They had to change their perspective about Whitney Brown. Reed Price, the strong advocate for Whitney, could no longer ignore the harmful behavior of his beloved pastor and confronted him.

To recognize and treat a problem as an adaptive challenge will rock the emotional boat. Leaders cannot expect members to change without objection. People expect their leaders to offer certainty, not to disturb them with unknowns. Likewise, people expect their leaders to secure order rather than confront them with disturbing choices. Congregational members expect their leaders to supply straightforward solutions that will quickly restore balance. When leaders treat problems as adaptive ones, they receive few accolades from members. But without the willingness to challenge people's expectations of quick and easy solutions, a leader will be subservient to those expectations. People don't want leaders to upset them with adaptive solutions that involve change, learning, loss, and uncertainty. However, if no behavior pattern or viewpoint has significantly changed

it's ok to challenge status quo, or problems may worsen

and deep problems have not been addressed, the problems will persist and the boat must be rocked.

Many excellent examples of the technical/adaptive understanding of problems come from medical history. Sherwin Nuland, clinical professor of surgery at Yale University, tells the incredible story of how medicine confused these two types of problems in the longstanding treatment of an illness. For thousands of years, women were dying of a fever at childbirth. The prevailing opinion about its cause was so entrenched that new theories were ridiculed or easily dismissed. Here's the setting:

The physicians and nurses caring for the girl were all too familiar with the disease that took her young life. In 1847, one of every six mothers, like this young woman, was dying in the First Division of the Allgemeine Krankenhaus. The experience in this Vienna hospital was not unique; it was happening in hospitals throughout Europe. Childhood fever was rampant.

Twenty-two hundred years before, the disease had been described in the Hippocratic volume called *Epidemics*. Even at that time, the cause of the disease was thought to be found in some stagnant or putrefied material whose source was within the body of the patient herself. An examiner of the disease, Dr. John Clarke (1793) referred to the disease as puerperal fever (*puer* = "child" and *parare* = "to bring forth"), believing it was contagious, though this represented a minority viewpoint.

Oliver Wendell Holmes undertook a study of the problem of the transmission of the fever, thinking it had infectious qualities and that physicians might be one of the carriers. But he was dismissed when an older doctor called his study "the meandering of a sophomore."

Puerperal fever continued to ravage the lives of young mothers because no one recognized the source—the hands of the physicians battling to prevent it. Doctors prior to delivery would examine cadavers and, because they did not sterilize their hands, they would bring foul particles from the lab to the clinic.

Ignac Semmelweiss started a new procedure, requiring medical students to wash their hands in a sanitizing solution before making an examination of the mother-to-be. The mortality rate declined. He published his results in a book that was rejected because his observation contradicted current medical beliefs, which blamed disease not on germs but to an imbalance of the "humors" in the body. Trivializing Semmelweiss's claims, the supervisor of the Allgemeine Krankenhaus attributed the improvement in statistics to a new ventilating system in the hospital. The situation required an adaptive response (integrating new learning) but received a technical one (the ventilating system). If Semmelweiss's theory had held in medical practice at that time, those who had believed otherwise would have experienced losses and casualties, such as credibility and authority.[4]

Resistance to Adaptive Change

Some members of the 19th-century European medical establishment had become so invested in their theory that new evidence could not be tolerated. "Adaptive change stimulates resistance," note Heifetz and Linsky, "because it challenges people's habits, beliefs, and values."[5] The medical establishment's beliefs about the cause of disease would have been jeopardized. Congregations will put up a struggle against taking new action, but also will struggle against believing embarrassing news, upsetting messages, and shocking reports. When leaders upset the emotional system, they can't be surprised if people think their ideas are like "the meandering of a sophomore" or if people dismiss them by referring to their version of the Allgemeine Krankenhaus ventilating system. At highly anxious times, people regress. Their survival patterns are established, very little is negotiable. Once the amygdala learns its lessons, learning stops. Employing primitive defense mechanisms, the agitated can see red but cannot see clearly. Though we may charge these resisters with being narrow-minded or parochial, they represent a human truth. No one likes to change because loss of some type will occur.

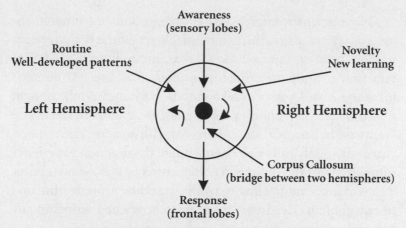

Awareness
(sensory lobes)

Routine
Well-developed patterns

Novelty
New learning

Left Hemisphere

Right Hemisphere

Corpus Callosum
(bridge between two hemispheres)

Response
(frontal lobes)

The Left and Right Hemispheres of the Brain

Returning to an examination of the functioning of the brain, we can better understand how natural it is to resist change. Our neocortex (thinking brain) is divided into two hemispheres, which play different but complimentary roles in learning. The right hemisphere is the hemisphere of novelty, exploration, and the unfamiliar; the left hemisphere is the hemisphere of routine, the storage of useful knowledge, and the known. All learning, therefore, begins on the right and proceeds to the left. One of the important questions that looms for the brain is, "Have I confronted this before?" If it has not, the right hemisphere of the brain, organized fundamentally to process novelty, will light up. On sight of a friend, the left hemisphere of the brain becomes active. Brain imaging will show a trained musician processing music in the left hemisphere and a novice activating the right hemisphere.

> I know that most men . . . can seldom accept even the simplest and most obvious truth if it be such as would oblige them to admit the falsity of conclusions which they have delighted in explaining to colleagues, which they have proudly taught to others, and which they have woven, thread by thread, into the fabric of their lives.
>
> —Leo Tolstoy, 19th-century Russian writer[6]

Neuroscientist Elkhonon Goldberg notes in his book *The Wisdom Paradox* that the two hemispheres of the brain interact with each other, but each one has a unique function. The interaction is more noticeable in women than men. Goldberg's ideas about the hemispheres are not the ones commonly thought of—that is, "left-brain" people are linear and logical while "right-brain" people are creative and disorderly. He reports that individuals with right hemisphere dysfunction experience difficulty with the unknown. They "usually eschew novel situations. They tend to cling to routines and be rigid, fearful, and resentful of any departure from well-entrenched scripts in any life circumstances."[7]

Goldberg's observation is corroborated by the experience of Kurt Goldstein, a neurologist who worked with right-brain injuries during World War II. His patients exhibited little capacity for imagination. They kept their closets in definite order. The patients placed their shoes and shirts in specific places. If their closets were disturbed, the patients panicked. The patients could not make a new arrangement or imagine a fresh order. They simply couldn't process new messages through the left brain.[8]

When the right hemisphere processes new information, it stacks the information up against what is already known. To classify the new, our brains compare it to old recipes, known scripts, and familiar categories stored in the left hemisphere. Over time, it is neurologically simple to become set in our thinking, especially if we are never exposed to something new. Some people seem to prefer specific rules for living that they can memorize and store in their left hemisphere, never having to hassle with ambiguity or uncertainties in the right hemisphere.

Adaptive change involves stimulation of the right hemisphere. Complicating matters, the right hemisphere not only processes new information but also our negative emotions—like frustration, anxiety, and anger. Meanwhile the left hemisphere is active with positive feelings such as love. No wonder that the known and the familiar are pleasing to most, while what is new

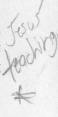

can be irritating or intimidating. The familiar associates with pleasurable feelings. The unknown is scary. When we look at how Jesus taught, we recognize that much of what he was saying involved adaptive change. He appealed to the right hemisphere, inviting brainstorming and encouraging imagination. In the story of the good Samaritan (Luke 10:29–37), for instance, he didn't cite a dictionary definition of the neighbor (left brain). He went straight to his listeners' right hemisphere asking, "Can you imagine a Samaritan caring for a Jew?" When the Gospel writers told the story of Jesus's encounter with the rich young ruler (Mark 10:17–22), Jesus didn't exclaim, "Great work, son! You're the most noble example of ethical living in the land. You've kept all the rules." Instead, he shocked him with the challenge to sell all he possessed and give the profits to the poor. The rich young ruler's right hemisphere was spinning. This ethical idea didn't square off with any commandment he knew. Jesus also healed on the Sabbath. He openly challenged the fixed law, because he could imagine that love superceded code. He encouraged those who were offended to use their imagination: "The sabbath was made for humankind, and not humankind for the sabbath" (Mark 2:27). Beginning a sermon, Jesus stated, "You have heard that it was said, . . . But I say unto you . . ." (Matt. 5). Within minutes, he probably lost the left-hemisphere listeners. And when he said, "The meek will inherit the earth" (Matt. 5:5), no left-hemisphere brain would ever accept that nonsense. Jesus challenged the routine and regimentation of the established order. Prophets deal with "adaptive" work.

A Personal Note

Your willingness to question, your eagerness to keep the congregation in alignment with its purposes, your deep appreciation for the life of the congregation, your courage to speak the truth in love, your capacity to take a position based on principle—all of it can slowly drain away. If you rock the emotional boat, you can expect an emotional reaction. You may be isolated, belittled, and replaced.

The joys of leadership have a counterpart in the pains of leadership. It is the pain that restrains many people in exercising leadership. Leaders have a built-in supply of remedies that will defend them—numbing anxiety, retaliating, quitting, nurturing cynicism, to name a few.

Leadership always involves a "double-blind bind." "Protect us," members of a community affirm, "and provide us with direction," as long as protection and direction don't involve rocking the emotional boat and challenging the community with some adaptive change for which members must take responsibility. It's a catch-22: protect and direct still holds as the expectation of leaders, but not if it means uncertainty, loss, and pain.

Self-management is critical, even more so in the boat-rocking times. Your calm, reflective, and principle-based action can be as infectious as anxiety. While anxiety spreads fast, the effects of a thoughtful approach are slower but eventually more effective and beneficial.

The Leader's Notebook

An Intervention with a Congregation

I have completed more than 150 interventions with troubled congregations, spanning 20 years. In addition, I have assisted seminaries, hospitals, judicatories, and church agencies in the same period. In anxious times, the same behaviors and interactions are present regardless of the setting. Living systems resemble one another.

A typical intervention involves the following elements:
A congregation invites me to help because its emotional boat is rocking. People are standing in the boat taking sides, only to tilt the congregation back and forth. They want to restore stability, therefore the opponents decide to sit down

and bring in a neutral third party. For months they have tried all kinds of technical fixes, yet the problem persists. There is hardly a church conflict that doesn't require an adaptive change.

The request for my services comes after the realization that the congregation is not making progress toward breaking the tense deadlock. I am invited to describe what I would do to help the congregation or other system in dealing with its dilemma. In most instances, they interview three or four possible consultants, then choose one.

If selected, I meet to inform the congregation leadership of the time involvement (three to four months), costs, and process. I am careful to outline what I expect of them and what they can expect of me (what I will and will not do). I list what they may expect as possible outcomes.

I never know in advance what the results will be. I have been surprised both ways: high expectations for good outcomes are sometimes not met; low expectations are sometimes far surpassed, exceeding what I thought could happen. Results are rarely immediate. They are discernable only months later. With every congregation, I make it clear that the process will continue beyond my presence with them.

I do not promise a return to normalcy to contain their anxiety. If anything, I am aware that my intervention will rock the boat again. I promise to use a structured and tested process that has as its goal to induce learning, first by defining clearly the problem and then exploring to find solutions. I understand conflict to be a resource for learning. When people are reflective instead of reflexive, they will be more open to adaptive challenges. This approach assumes that I manage the processes by which people with the problem achieve the resolution. They are the experts.

In this process I will be sabotaged, and I tell them that. Someone or some group will attempt to impede progress. One way to reduce my influence is by "neutralizing" me.

Actually, I don't mind sabotage because it's a sign that the process, to some degree, is effective and some anxious people are worried that things aren't going their way. Sabotage might include statements such as, "He's a pastor who favors pastors" or "He doesn't understand our congregation." Sabotage might include actions such as members stacking the deck at focus groups or violating ground rules that have been established.

Even though the process is designed to lead them to make decisions, many people still think I am there to solve their problems. They interpret the problem as a technical one, and I am the expert who knows how to remedy it. No matter how many times I reiterate that my role is to conduct a process to assist the congregation in formulating choices for itself, a good number still adhere to the notion that I am there to tell them what to do, to make it right, to make it like it was before, or to make them feel better. I can never challenge enough the idea that church conflict is a technical problem. In anxious times, a good number of people fall into "functional helplessness"—that is, while they want to be rescued by my recommendations, I want them to be empowered by their own choices.

I am explicit in noting that I will be upfront, specific, and frank. I don't lighten people's anguish with "soft reporting." I lay out what people tell me, as is. This is distressing for some. But as my mentor Edwin Friedman said to me: "Your reporting is directed to the most mature people." Those who are more concerned with feelings than facts may become angry with me. For some, my written report to the congregation will bring reaction, resistance, and emotional outbursts.

Other people are grateful for having the situation clarified so that it can be addressed. Clarity isn't always comforting, however, especially if it upsets people's viewpoints, allegiances, or expectations. Again, even though I am careful to mention that my report is intended for *action,* people tend to see it as an *evaluation.*

The Action Report, as I call it, is merely a reflection of what people have told me. I gather information through four means, such as personal interviews and written responses. From the responses, I isolate three to five key issues, describing each one briefly. To engender thinking, I raise seven to eight questions specific to the congregation's situation. There will be pain for some people. But some pain can't be worked through without a period in which that pain is deepened. Growth will follow.

From Edwin Friedman I have learned that if a person is going to take the lead in an intervention process, he needs to have some measure of tolerance for pain in others (as well as in himself), believing that pain can be a teacher and motivator. And a person needs to understand that when she stimulates pain in others, they will react in return. Without a deepening of pain, growth seldom happens. Even more, leaders have to give people the freedom not to learn from their own experience. In anxious times, with the emotional boat rocking, learning doesn't always happen, but it's the only hope that something may change.

Chapter 9

To Challenge or to Survive

In this chapter we will look at two types of leadership, one that provides security and one that takes risks.

Congregational leadership is an extraordinary opportunity. Through your service, you help address the needs of people and direct their energies toward a common purpose. You draw people's attention to something larger than themselves. In highly anxious times, people become more demanding about their needs and leaders are tested in new ways. The common purpose you share becomes diffused. The larger view is lost in the pressure of the moment.

Even beyond these anxious periods, a leader has to contend with normal stresses. The notion that authority cannot be trusted is prevalent today. Leaders are regularly criticized. People in any organization settle into a comfort zone and refuse to budge. People's expectations of you reach unrealistic proportions—keep everyone's spirit high, discourage any negative talk, stay loyal to the community's values, eliminate vexing questions, maintain calm for the sake of togetherness. Sometimes the expectation is, "Remember, you are not authorized to push us, quiz us, or surprise us. If you want to be liked, don't get ahead of us. Be our leader, but keep following us." The leader is effectively neutralized.

Leadership brings you assaults and roadblocks. Yet leadership doesn't mean that you have to sacrifice yourself or be sacrificed by someone else. Leadership has many other possibilities. No doubt, periods of stress bring on automatic survival needs. Instincts take over. The protective part of the brain is in control. Once the environment feels safe again, a new imperative—to stretch and push forward—may emerge. No choice is more important than whether you choose to be a leader who gets bogged down in survival or one who rises to the level of challenge. Are you driven by the impulsive reactions of others or your own survival instincts? Do you serve thoughtfully and courageously?

The biblical story of two brothers, Moses and Aaron, leading the Israelites through the wilderness provides a context to explore the difference between the leader who enjoys adventure and the leader who automatically "makes nice" or worries about preserving the peace. At a dramatic point in Israel's history, we see Moses accepting challenge and Aaron committing to survival.

Two Brothers

The people of Israel are free! God has delivered them from the oppression of Pharaoh. This event's immense significance is reflected in the celebration of the exodus centuries later by generations of the Israelites' descendants. "Free at last! Free at last!" But these early days in the wilderness are harsh and anxiety-ridden. Imagine leading a large band of former slaves through an endless rocky, grim terrain. The burden of life as Egyptian slaves has ended. Now oppression comes from hunger, thirst, and exhaustion. The food is monotonous, the nights are cold, the days are uneventful.

Miles away from the Red Sea, the people come to Elim and, for the moment, they enjoy a place where twelve springs and seventy palms form an oasis. How refreshing and satisfying! They could not stay long, however, because the journey lay ahead. Quickly, the first huge hassle begins: Then "the whole congregation of the Israelites complained against Moses and Aaron . . . 'for you have brought us out into this wilderness to kill this whole assembly with hunger'" (Exod. 16:2–3). It's a crisis of basic human need coupled with the stress that there is no visible evidence the need will be met. Nevertheless, God hears the pleading cry of the assembly and responds immediately.

In the minds of these desert refugees, the empty landscape is a place of struggle and threat. And as people do in hard times, they look to their leadership for relief. Being in a sour mood, they question the leadership ability of the two brothers. Both of them have been the targets of the people's unhappiness before. In Egypt, in reaction to Moses's request to release the people from slavery, Pharaoh had upped the ante and increased the people's burdens—"Make more bricks." The people complained to Moses: "You have brought us into bad odor with Pharaoh and his officials" (Exod. 5:21). To comfort the people, Moses recited the promises of God's mercy, but "they would not listen to Moses, because of their broken spirit and their cruel slavery" (6:9).

Now, once again, tempers flare in the dreary desert. "Our wives and our children and our cattle are thirsty" (17:3, author paraphrase). Bowed and beaten, Moses himself complains to God that the people are ready to stone him. What else can he do?

Then the fateful event happens. The people's physical weariness turns into spiritual despair. They have had enough of this God of Abraham, Isaac, and Jacob. Moses has been gone for forty days and forty nights, which in biblical terms means a long time. He's nowhere in sight. Like a thundering herd, the congregation descends on Aaron: "Come, make gods for us, who shall go before us" (32:1). Under the intense pressure of the moment, Aaron reacts. With his amygdala excited in milliseconds, Aaron takes the low road (hasty and thoughtless). We might wonder how Aaron could join this frenzied mob. No resistance. No discussion. No caution that the people need to reflect on things before acting. Yielding instantly to their feverish anxiety, he offers them a quick fix. Out of the melted golden jewelry, Aaron shapes a golden calf to satisfy the people's need for tangible assurance. What a failure of nerve!

On his return, Moses sees that the people are out of control. Incredulous, Moses looks for Aaron. "What did this people do to you," Moses asks, "that you have brought so great a sin upon them?" (32:21). Aaron, so pitifully spineless, takes no responsibility. "You know the people, that they are bent on evil" (v. 22). Essentially, Aaron is saying he acted under stress. "They made me do it" is his excuse. In addition, Aaron claims he merely threw the glittering jewels into the fire and the form of a golden calf appeared. How is that for self-serving spinning? He never admits he had shaped it. Notice, too, he makes no mention that he designed and built an altar for sacrifices. He is silent about his invitation to the excited crowd to come back the next day for a foot-stomping festival. Actually, the Hebrew word for this feast, *tschak,* means "to laugh." To Moses this was no laughing scene, however, and he melts and crushes the gold used to construct the calf, sprinkles the pulverized metal in water, and makes the people drink it.

Major Differences

Although of the same flesh, the two brothers function so differently. Moses has more of a "solid self." Murray Bowen defined a solid self as a self that is not negotiable to satisfy what others want of us. Not Aaron—he's soft as putty. He's everybody's friend. Aaron is willing to be the way others want him to be. First he pimps gods to these half-hearted believers. Then, to sweeten the deal, he appeals to their party-animal instincts with a spur-of-the-moment blast. To cement their approval of him, he exceeds their demands and adds a bonus, erecting an altar for sacrifices. Bowen called this negotiable self the "pseudo-self."[1] Colloquially, we depict this behavior as being chameleon-like, being someone's "poodle," or lacking a backbone. A pseudo-self is created by emotional pressure. The person simply is overly sensitive to others' opinions and too willing to do what others want him or her to do; the person adapts quickly to gain praise and avoid criticism. Who can tell where Aaron begins and ends and where others do? He is emotionally fused with them. As metals lose their characteristics in a blazing fire, Aaron loses self in pandering to the people. In fused relationships, everything flows into everything else. It's a psychological stew. In fusion, there is nothing to come up against. There are no contrasts.

Without contrasts, a person's sense perception is skewed, as in a painting with no figure and ground to create depth. Understanding is distorted without difference. To paraphrase Plato: How can we comprehend anything if there are not two contraries to awaken reflection? Words need to be combined with other words to make sense. Unless we connect two sounds, they don't make a melody. No less, relationships require contrasts—that is, separate parts that connect. Fusion is not connection. It is absorption.

A self that is negotiable is a self without principles. A pseudo-self takes a position determined by others. Aaron capitulates to the people's fickleness. By selling his soul in exchange for people's approval, he becomes a "host cell" to their desire. Too busy taking care of people's feelings, functioning to relieve them of their frustrations, he does not stop to think and offer a contrast to their emotionality. He does not differentiate himself.

Differentiation? In this story, we have to look to Moses for some evidence of it. When God invites Moses to lead the children of Israel out of Egypt, Moses stands up, saying, "Me, I am not an orator, I stutter" (Exod. 4:10). Bold enough to argue thoughtfully with God, Moses is no emotional pushover. Later when God becomes utterly disgusted with the Israelites in the desert, God decides to change people, not the leader. Again, Moses rises to the occasion and intercedes on behalf of the Israelites. After Aaron automatically surrenders to the people's emotional pressure for a tangible, visual god, Moses holds no grudge against his brother for a monumental failure. He forgives him and stays connected.

Strangely, Moses and Aaron, seen by the people as coleaders, don't receive equal treatment. All the blame is spread before the feet of Moses, never Aaron. If the people were about to stone Moses, why is Aaron not subject to the same consequence? Moses doesn't complain about the unfairness. And he doesn't try to win the people's favor. Without hesitation, he confronts the congregation for its failures. Often solitary and alone, Moses never abandons the congregation (though he would have liked to have done that on a couple of occasions). Moses has the ability to stay connected with people even when they are emotionally upset. Moses expresses a solid self that is not negotiable in relationships because it is grounded in principle. He has the courage to keep going forward in spite of wretched

conditions and critical opposition. Moses understands that he cannot control the passion and action of these former slaves. He can, however, choose his own response to them, despite the fact that the choices they make are not the ones he would have chosen for them.

Surely Moses has his reactive moments. His portrait in the Old Testament is balanced. His shortcomings and his strengths appear. He pounds the tablets on the ground, breaking them into pieces. He screams at God: "I am not able to carry all this people alone, for they are too heavy for me. If this is the way you are going to treat me, put me to death at once . . . and do not let me see my misery" (Num. 11:14–15). Ultimately, Moses refuses to let survival substitute for challenge. In the face of pressure from anxious forces, Moses remains committed to the long term.

Nobel Peace Prize winner Elie Wiesel says that Moses has enough of a self to argue (to take a stand). Aaron never does. "He accepts everything from everybody."[2] Moses knows that leaders inevitably fail someone. That, however, doesn't prevent Moses from taking action. "Moses fights battles and loses some," Wiesel says, "but never gives up or gives in, whereas Aaron runs away from any violent confrontation." Wiesel concludes: "Moses is a fervent believer in truth, just as Aaron is in peace—in peace above all."[3]

Moses represents the leader who is willing to challenge. Aaron portrays the leader who does what is necessary to survive, lets whatever the polls say determine his behavior, and maintains stability even if it means losing self. Moses doesn't accept the fact that, although the people had seen firsthand God at work in their lives, they had not learned anything. Aaron? He's smiling, ready to yield to any passion to preserve harmony. Learning is too messy, too slow. He chooses to be a leader who follows.

The Pressure and the Pattern

The congregation of Israel is a reflection of any congregation caught in the grip of emotional processes. When anxiety is high, resorting to more automatic functioning is normal for people. Since nature has prepared us to be afraid of real or imagined threats, we are innately designed to avoid danger. We turn to our survival instincts. The amygdala incites anxious reactions. Once our primitive survival brain rules, we are driven to reflexive behaviors. At the same time, our reflective capacities are constricted, limiting the range of responses we might make. All the advantages a left prefrontal cortex provides—hindsight, insight, and foresight—seem to be lost at once.

Only when automatic processes are interrupted in some way are the automatic outcomes changed. Only when we see the crisis before us as not simply a matter of survival but also a matter of challenge is adaptive change possible. But adaptive change requires a period of disorientation—a formless void. We don't know what is coming next. We find ourselves in the strange wilderness. The safe, known world with all of its pleasurable feelings is gone for a time, and not until we live out that time do we come to a new beginning—a reorientation.

When people stagger in this no-man's-land, three patterns form: the instant solution, the short-term fix, and adaptive change.

Pattern One: The Instant Solution

Under great pressure, congregations destabilize. A series of unfavorable events suddenly or rapidly occurs. Anxiety intensifies and spreads. Behaviors are predictable: faulting others, denying the seriousness of the problem, avoiding others who disagree with us, and demanding swift resolution.

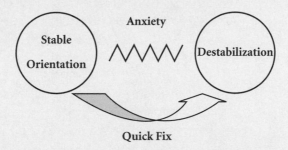

Quick Fix

In the quick-fix scenario, leaders act in a placating or rescuing manner to extinguish the flame of reactivity. They do not get outside the anxious system to take thoughtful stands. They sacrifice learning for the comfort of the moment and the rapid return to stability.

Pattern Two: The Short-Term Fix

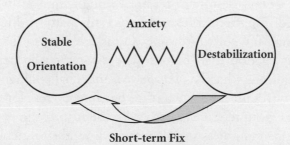

Short-term Fix

As the anxiety-driven processes escalate in a mindless fashion, leaders get a little distance from the stress and slow down their responses. They feel a sense of urgency but not panic. The ultimate aim is to reduce people's anxiety in the short term (let the dust settle, cool things down). But no one gets to the root of the problem. Learning still does not happen because the leader's prime objective is anxiety's reduction.

Pattern Three: Adaptive Change

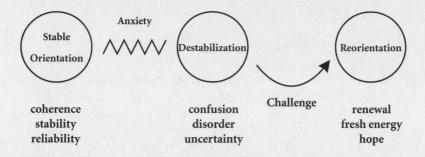

coherence	confusion	renewal
stability	disorder	fresh energy
reliability	uncertainty	hope

For leaders to act on the courage of their convictions rather than on the power of their feelings takes time. Yet courage enables leaders to resist those who insist on immediate relief or who want others to take care of things in order to excuse themselves from making a tough decision or taking responsibility. Adaptive change is possible because people are willing to hold back the tendency to revert to the old way of reactivity and to learn new responses.

When a congregation becomes destabilized, the two automatic ways to restore order are through survival behaviors, evidenced in patterns one and two. Only pattern three, however, allows for new learning. Why is learning so important? If a congregation does not use the disorientation period for understanding what has happened and challenging itself to take steps to shift the system, the chances are great for patterns one and two to repeat themselves in the future. No emotional system changes unless people change how they function with one another.

Challenge or Survival

Challenge leaders are quite different from survival leaders. For challenge leaders, adaptive change is primary. On the other hand, survival leaders are safety focused. "The safest place for

Challenge Leaders	Survival Leaders
Take thoughtful action	Take expedient action based on emotional pressures
Risk goodwill for the sake of truth	Play it safe for the benefit of preserving stability
Stay the course (hold steady)	Use quick fixes for restoring harmony
Manage self	Find scapegoats to blame, look outside of self for rescuing

ships is in the harbor," Edwin Friedman wrote, "but that's not why ships were built."[4] Leaders are chosen to lead—with all the risk that may involve. The chart above compares the behavior of these two types of leaders. To explore each of the behaviors on the challenge side, I use the narratives below in the context of congregational life.

Take Thoughtful Action

University Church situated near the campus of a state university attracts less than half the number of people it did in its peak years. Those who participate in worship, nurture, and service are committed individuals. About 150 people are actively engaged in parish life. Two pastors serve University: Diane Brock, age 48, and Michael Lofton, age 32. Their relationship is well defined by clear boundaries about roles and expectations. Diane provides direction and inspiration; Michael is the nurturer and caretaker. In the five years she has been senior pastor, Diane has led the congregation in becoming a significant contributor to a number of collaborative ministries with other Christians.

When Diane proposed that the congregation begin a study of family values, believing that churches like University had left the issue to the more conservative churches, Jeff Frazier, a university professor, and two graduate students vociferously opposed the study. They claimed the issue was a bogus one, invented by groups seeking political advantage. Since very little has disturbed the congregation, the sudden puffed-up anxiety that exploded came as a surprise.

Diane was perplexed. Initially she thought Jeff's obstinate opposition was nothing but obstinate opposition, maybe to deepen the discussion. When Jeff's adamant position was fortified by anger, Diane became upset. His hostile demeanor seemed out of proportion to the issue.

The parties finally agreed to submit the issue to arbitration. Three people agreed to mediate—Charlie Wagner, the council president; a pastor from another congregation who had mediation training; and a layperson from the community at large. Complicating the matter, however, was the fact that Jeff Frazier was African American. Several people feared that if Jeff didn't get his way, he would play the race card. Never before had this happened in the congregation, but Jeff had once accused others at the university of being racist when he failed to get his way.

When the mediation ended, Charlie Wagner announced that the pastor had the right to introduce new concerns and if others objected, they could invest themselves in the many other study and outreach programs of the congregation. Charlie acknowledged Jeff's right to oppose the family-values study, but believed the case had been resolved through the arbitration process. But Jeff Frazier didn't see it that way. His new attacks focused on Charlie Wagner.

Charlie worked for a foundation that gave grants to nonprofit organizations. Jeff let it be known that Charlie had no minorities working at the foundation and that a disproportionate number of foundation grants for minority programs were rejected. Angry, Charlie wanted to counterattack. He looked for Jeff at church but couldn't find him. He called and sent e-mail. No response.

On second thought, Charlie decided not to pounce on Jeff. "If I do that," he said to himself, "I'd be defensive." Instead, Charlie Wagner sent Jeff an e-mail, saying he had heard about *prudent*

Jeff's comments and that he wanted to meet with Jeff to hear suggestions he might have to improve minority representation at the foundation. For weeks there was no response and no sign of Jeff at church. Meanwhile Diane, frustrated with Jeff, made no effort to contact him.

Late one Friday afternoon as Charlie was locking his office door, Jeff appeared, asking Charlie if they could talk. They went into Charlie's office. A disconsolate Jeff revealed that his wife, who was white, had had a brief affair with another man, who was white. Jeff had spent weeks plotting his revenge. Now, however, vengeance had lost its appeal. Jeff wanted to work on his marriage, and he believed his wife, Brenda, would be willing to join him in therapy.

On Sunday, Charlie reported his encounter with Jeff to Diane. Though saddened by the news of Jeff's marital problems, Diane still had to ask, "Did he ever apologize?" Charlie shook his head no and added, "Diane, I don't know if Jeff even remembered what happened six weeks ago. He was an emotional wreck." Several days later Diane sent an e-mail to Charlie: "From *The Nicomachean Ethics of Aristotle*: Anybody can become angry—that is easy. But to be angry with the right person, to the right degree, at the right time, for the right purpose, and in the right way—that is not easy."[5]

By controlling his impulse to pounce on Jeff, Charlie took a more reasonable course and invited Jeff into a conversation about his concerns, which Jeff accepted later but for a different purpose. Stepping back, observing, and taking the neurological high road, Charlie opened space for something other than an eye-for-an-eye or fighting fire with fire. Reacting to reactivity produces heat, not light. We can give up self by not disturbing the peace and by taking care of others' feelings, but we can just as easily do it by uncorking the primitive passions and not regulating them. Charlie nearly acted on his first impulse but couldn't find Jeff at church. Charlie then had second thoughts—allowing him to consider the appropriateness of his emotionality and to control the course of his reactions. Attentive to his own functioning, Charlie chose not to allow his reactivity to go toe-to-toe with Jeff's. Instead he took thoughtful action.

Risk Goodwill

Two leaders at St. Andrew's Church, Tom Tucker and Diane O'Meara, met privately with Pastor Foster McKinney to notify him that a young girl in the church had accused him of molestation. By state law they were compelled to report the incident to a governmental agency. Foster shook his head in disbelief and quietly said, "I have never touched her. Never." Tom and Diane suggested that Foster take a leave of absence. Foster wasn't sure what to do. "I need to clear my name," he responded, "but I don't want to drag St. Andrew's through this for months and months." After consulting with some people, Foster announced that he would not take a leave of absence, lest it be seen as indication of guilt. At first the leaders were wary of his decision, fearful of the consequences for the congregation. After the congregation had been informed, naturally a group of members thought he should leave. The leadership, however, decided to stand beside him and to let the process of justice unfold. They were warned that most cases like this one are based in fact. The charges are not frivolous.

The leaders met weekly for a prayer vigil followed by a sharing time in which the leaders openly expressed what they were thinking. Tom Tucker mentioned that he simply trusted his intuition that Foster was innocent. Meanwhile Diane O'Meara had questions about the young girl's stability and the circumstances in which the molestation was to have taken place. The girl's parents had gone through a turbulent divorce two years ago but now had jointly hired an attorney. Another leader confessed that she was ready to withdraw her support from McKinney because of the pressure she felt from other members. Foster told everyone he appreciated their support, but if they wanted to withdraw their support of him, he would harbor no resentment. One member of the council did resign. Another council member, Marie Briggs, stood steadfast with Foster because she had been falsely accused of something in her own work situation.

"Sure, I wondered if Foster did something," Diane said, "and I wondered, 'What if I'm wrong about my belief in his innocence?'" During the weekly gatherings, Diane reported some frank discussions between Foster McKinney and the executive committee. "We didn't smell a rat," Diane reported, "because Foster wasn't defensive and gave permission to anyone to doubt him." Foster had a reputation for being a peace and justice pastor. A few anxious people turned that against him, mocking his stance as a camouflage for aberrant behavior. They had Foster condemned. Marie Briggs stood up for Foster because he had been a strong proponent of justice. "We can't let people's assumptions sentence this good man," she asserted, "I was unfairly treated in my job, even accused of inappropriate behavior. The very same behavior my supervisor was doing to me." She thought the least the congregation could do is to let the justice process run its course.

Fourteen weeks later, the charges were suddenly dropped. Buoyed by the news, Tom and Diane gathered the leaders for a response to the changed situation. Both volunteered to visit all the members they knew who were doubters or who had pulled back, assuring them they were welcome to return—no questions, no judgments.

Rarely have I seen the courage of this leadership team at St. Andrew's. It didn't happen because of blind allegiance to McKinney or the pressure leaders felt to act as one. The full reality of doubt and belief, suspicion and trust, anxiety and clarity became part of their discernment process. Under these stressful conditions, many people become what psychologists call "cognitive misers." They think instinctively of either/or—either innocent or guilty, either bad or good. Excruciating as the process had been for them, the leaders at St. Andrew's came to a position that allowed all possibilities to exist. As heroic as that may sound, they were also vilified and assailed by those who wanted to take the path of least resistance and remove Foster McKinney. But the leaders operated on the principle that the truth needed to be told before the judgment could be rendered.

Stay the Course

Wayne and Sandra Rogers were the new copastors at Bethel. They had been in their new setting only a couple of weeks. Their assignment was to turn around or to revitalize an eighty-year-old congregation. At its peak in the 1960s, Bethel had 300 members. Slow but steady attrition had left them with nearly 90 members. Most members were committed to the congregation through long-standing family ties. The neighborhood had been undergoing a change in population for five years. An African-American community brackets one side of the church and a multiracial group the other side. The white members drove eight to twenty-five miles to come to Bethel.

One late afternoon as Wayne finished painting the front porch of the parsonage, next door to the church sanctuary, several black youth about ten to twelve years old came into the yard. They asked Roger if the church was going to have a summer camp. Unaware of such a program, Wayne asked the boys if the congregation had sponsored one before. They said they didn't know but that having a summer camp was easy: all that was needed were permission slips.

Wayne told Sandra about his conversation with the boys. She said, "Let's do it." They planned a two-week summer camp and invited the boys. Twelve youngsters attended. The following summer the number increased to 60. More important, the summer camp opened the door to the immediate neighborhood. On the negative side, members started to leave as Wayne and Sandra led the congregation to more direct contact with the immediate community. Financial support decreased as well. To help the congregation financially, Wayne and Sandra moved into a small apartment, making it possible to rent out the parsonage for income. They made personal sacrifices by accepting a salary reduction. Things started to turn around financially when the estate of Selena Montoya, a long-time member, was donated to Bethel.

The anxious times could have easily produced quick fixes, but Wayne and Sandra Rogers were determined to go through the anxious times because they had a vision of what could happen. Rather than allowing anxiety to determine their responses, they stayed the course. Challenge leaders have the capacity to give power to the future in contrast to survival leaders who give power to the past or to the present.

Managing Self

We are back once again to where we began—the capacity to self-manage: to think before we act; to observe ourselves; to define ourselves by saying, "I think" or "I believe"; to resist cutting off from or giving in to others; to focus on our own behavior.

The final story I will share in this chapter is a personal one involving my work with a large congregation composed of many educated people. In a letter to the personnel committee, 14 of the 16 staff members expressed major dissatisfaction with the senior pastor. The letter was leaked to outside sources and distributed to many members. The senior pastor accused one staff member of being the culprit who disseminated what was to be an in-house communication. The person charged actually did not release it, but the accusation emotionally stung her and she resigned. Those who benefited from her ministry began to organize a group to strike back against her accuser. Meanwhile several elected leaders had no patience with the staff and privately told some of them to leave. The conditions worsened: finances started to decline; rumors were coming from many sides; the leaders were slow to address the issues. A few months passed before the leaders contacted me to work with the congregation; the plot had only thickened with new accusations and exaggerations.

I did my preliminary research with members of the congregation in preparation for giving them the Action Report, which includes the major issues confronting the congregation. When the day arrived for my reporting, I entered a room that could not handle the six- to seven-hundred people who attended, frustrating an already frustrated group. Waiting for the meeting to begin, I sat in a small office when a gentleman entered and said tartly: "If your report isn't favorable to the senior pastor, I'll see to it that your report is discredited." He left as suddenly as he had appeared. I later discovered that he was an extremely wealthy individual and influential with members of the congregation. Because the report listed facts and not blame, he later could only nitpick portions of it.

As I presented the report to the congregation, I was made aware of two mistakes in it, a mathematical one and a misattribution about who took a certain action. I mentioned, for instance, that 25 percent of the responses I received showed support for the senior pastor and 20 percent aligned themselves with the staff. I noted they were fighting for the backing of 45 percent among the uncommitted or neutral people. I didn't recognize that I had lost 10 percent in my mathematical counting—55 percent uncommitted or neutral people was the correct statistic. A statistician in the audience noticed it immediately and questioned the validity of the entire report. Further into the report my other mistake, the misattribution, surfaced. I had mixed up the identity of two sisters. I said "Mary" when I should have said "Martha." Not necessarily a significant mistake, except in this case the two sisters were on opposite sides of the controversy. This led to another comment that the report indicated a deficient understanding of the congregation, again to cast a shadow on its content. Many individuals were looking for a report that divided "the right" from "the wrong," depending on their perspective, not a report presenting a fair and objective perspective about what was happening.

My first impulse was to make light of my mistakes with a bit of humor. My defenses were working hard and I had to hold back the urge to exonerate myself. Instead, I said, "I made two mistakes. I hope these mistakes do not distract you from the important messages of this report. If the current polarization continues, you could be at this warring impasse for months and years." By defining myself rather than defending myself, I maintained my self-management. I am not always this emotionally resourceful. But I am aware that my self-regulation in the heat of the moment affects the whole system. Anxiety flows down and out from the center. As the leader of this process, I had to be in control of myself, especially if I wanted the Action Report to be a challenge for new learning in the congregation.

A Personal Note

Henri Nouwen, a renowned writer on spiritual living, suggested that if we are to be leaders who challenge, we can never forget that humility and courage are both necessary:

> There is within you a lamb and a lion. Spiritual maturity is the ability to let lamb and lion lie down together. Your lion is your adult, aggressive self. It is your initiative-taking and decision-making self. But there is also your fearful, vulnerable lamb, the part of you that will easily become a victim of your need for other people's attention. The art of spiritual living is to fully claim both your lion and your lamb. Then you can act assertively without denying your own needs. And you can ask for affection and care without betraying your talent to offer leadership.[6]

The lamb side needs connection for support, encouragement, and emotional uplift. Remember, the differentiated person is one who is always connected to others. Relationships count. The lamb's counterpart is the lion—the responsible adult side that believes in its ability to affect events that have an impact on people's lives, that takes responsibility for self (not blaming or scapegoating), that controls impulsive acts, that works through anxiety, that employs self-reflection before making decisions, that seeks objectivity when problems are knotty and complex, that takes clear, well-defined positions based on principles, and that values relationships.

Moving forward in the process of differentiation, the leader offers the congregation the opportunity of working creatively with (instead of reacting to) change and challenge. There are no guarantees that reactive forces won't derail or frustrate a leader's efforts. Nevertheless, the leader's functioning is not to be based on others' functioning.

You are called to lead. Nouwen wrote: "Developing your identity as a child of God in no way means giving up your responsibilities. Likewise, claiming your adult self in no way means that you cannot become increasingly a child of God. In fact, the opposite is true. The more you can feel safe as a child of God, the freer you will be to claim your mission in the world as a responsible human being."[7] Nouwen places the lamb and the lion together: the child and the adult; humility and courage; safety in being a son or daughter of God and freedom to lead.

The Leader's Notebook

A Word of Encouragement

Your ministry of leadership is grounded in the freeing gift of God's grace. In Christ, you are no longer a slave in bondage to fear. Knowing yourself to be accepted as a child of God, you are free to serve in love. As a responsible representative of God's love, you are free to take initiative to test your thoughts, to honor your intuition, to see what requires doing, and to accomplish it. You can be faithful to your task because you believe God is faithful to you. Anxious times test your wisdom, your patience, and your hope. But you draw courage, knowing,

> those who wait for the LORD shall renew their
>   strength,
> they shall mount up with wings like eagles,
> they shall run and not be weary,
> they shall walk and not faint.
>
> —Isaiah 40:31

Faith does not deliver you from the turmoil and unevenness of being human. You will continue to be tempted to conform to the pressure of the moment rather than to create a new future. You will continue to be fed by your own anxiety that fights against and stifles your freedom. The surprising and unpredictable wilderness—and the people's harping complaints—will continue to tap into your "Aaron instincts." You may not call it a golden calf, but your decision to please the masses, accepting their salvation schemes, has "golden calf" written all over it.

When you are tempted to give in, uncertain, or under the protection of your own automatic defenses, think of Psalm 27:

> The LORD is my light and my salvation;
> whom shall I fear?
> The LORD is the stronghold of my life;
> Of whom shall I be afraid?
> I believe that I shall see the goodness of the LORD

in the land of the living.
Wait for the LORD;
Be strong, and let your heart take courage;
Wait for the LORD!
                                        —Psalm 27:1, 13, 14

You might wonder if the psalmist is aware of how difficult it is to act in the way he proposes: to believe, wait, take courage, be strong. You might think to yourself that it's easy for him to urge that because he's never had to

- deal with a pastor who is depressed, refuses help, and only withdraws more after being confronted;
- work with a stubborn group of people who are withholding their offerings because the music director will not select their favorite hymns to sing;
- confront another leader who is acting imperially, as if she is not accountable to anyone;
- negotiate a way for an emotionally divided staff to come together, despite differences about the role of the new business manager;
- stretch people's thinking so that the congregation can adapt to shifting circumstances.

However, the psalmist is credible. He is no pious slacker plugging sweet advice on a blog. He himself looked rejection in the eye. He is acquainted with adversaries encircling him, with violence and war, with suffering unfair criticism, and even with betrayal by family members (vv. 2–3, 10, 12). These bold words—believe, wait, take courage, be strong—grow out of his own oppressions. The poet does not edit out the darkness or erase the data of despair.

"Let your heart take courage" is an invitation to become a participant in making a difference, here and now, in your congregation. The psalmist knows Doubt & Company firsthand. Believe, wait, take courage, be strong—they presuppose God's incredible faithfulness. Behind the encouragement is the assurance that God is for you:

> For he will hide me in his shelter in the day of trouble;
> he will conceal me under the cover of his tent;
> he will set me high on a rock.
>
> —Psalm 27:5

You are not asked to pull hope out of the thin air or to pump up your courage like a coach would inspire the team. You are not promised solutions. Instead, you are invited to have your strength renewed:

> For we do not have a high priest who is unable to sympathize with our weaknesses, but we have one who in every respect has been tested as we are, yet without sin. Let us therefore approach the throne of grace with boldness, so that we may receive mercy and find grace to help in time of need.
>
> —Hebrews 4:15, 16

For others to believe they will "see the goodness of the LORD in the land of the living" (Ps. 27:13) takes leaders who believe.

Postscript

People of the Charm

This postscript is an essay about narcissistic functioning as a systemic problem.[1] People who function in narcissistic ways require others' admiration. Likewise, those who supply the admiration need the certainty and flattery of the admired because he or she is special. The system is composed of two needy parts, each dependent on the other.

This system can exist in congregations where a self-absorbed and charming leader becomes the object of others' devotion. This essay describes the interaction between the charmer and the charmed and discusses some ways to address potential problems for congregations.

The Image

The term *narcissist* derives from the Greek myth of Narcissus. A young man named Narcissus is followed by a lovely mountain nymph, Echo, who is hopelessly in love with him. Calling to his companions, Narcissus shouts, "Let us come together here." Echo responds with the same words and rushes to embrace her love. But Narcissus frees himself from her grappling and runs away. He cries out, "I will die before you will ever be with me."

Echo is devastated. In addition to Narcissus's rejection of her, the gods, for a number of reasons, punish Echo. They leave her only a voice and condemn her to wander in oceans and valleys. Spurned, Echo seeks revenge. She asks the gods to punish Narcissus, making him the victim of unrequited love. So condemned, Narcissus falls in love with his own image in a pool and pines away because he can never possess it. Unable to pull himself away from the contemplation of his own beauty, he starves to death, falls into the water, and is never seen again. Narcissus's tragic flaw is that he can never love anyone else. His love of self inhibits coupling, fertility, and the giving of self.[2]

The narcissist must be given to. Psychiatrist James Masterson says: "The narcissist is motivated by the continuous need for 'supplies' to feed this grandiose conception of himself."[3] The narcissist functions to maintain a projected, inflated image of self. By coercing, charming, or controlling others, the narcissist ensures that the need for supplies will be satisfied. Functioning to mirror his grandiosity, others guarantee him a sense of specialness, exaggerated importance, and superiority.

Narcissistic Functioning

Some narcissism is normal, even healthy. Without it, no one could develop self-esteem or pursue unique ambitions. In contrast, pathological narcissism involves "excessive investment in self at the expense of investment in others."[4] The list below highlights the ways in which narcissistic functioning is unhealthy:

- The person is endlessly needy, wanting repetitive approval. He is over-dependent on external admiration and hungry for continuous narcissistic supplies, seeking mirroring from others to back up his own grandiosity.
- The person feels entitled to special consideration and is self-important (often exhibitionistic or dramatic to prove it).
- The person is capable of seeing only her perspective, is intolerant of disagreement, doesn't discuss ideas but imposes them, is single-minded, believes in her own superior wisdom, and doesn't need help from others.
- The person is ruthless toward those who do not reflect back his projected image of specialness. He is vindictive, vengeful, devaluing, and abrasive. He publicly humiliates others and wants others to be wholehearted supporters ("yes" people).

IT'S IMPORTANT FOR EVERYONE
TO REMEMBER... THIS IS ALL
ABOUT ME LOOKING GOOD

© Ray Johnson. Reprinted with permission.

- The person is prone to lying and is an expert at disguise.
- The person possesses little ability to control desires and lacks restraint, being impulsive and brash.
- The person displays an air of affability and self-confidence. He appears to be in command of situations, speaks with certainty, and has an aura of authority.
- The person presents herself impressively. She is clever, charming, seductive, persuasive, self-assured.
- The person acts defensively and shows no remorse. He has thick skin and a rigid front, denies weakness, and turns around something that fails or goes wrong, blaming circumstances on others or claiming innocence.
- The person is often likeable and impressive. He exhibits so-called star quality and can be fun to be with.
- The person is articulate and offers inspiring speeches that uplift people. He believes words can move mountains.
- The person is more interested in being admired than loved.
- The person is unable to use self-examination, is too self-engrossed to be self-observant, and does not fundamentally change.
- The person is obsessive about appearance (clothes, car, job position or title, location of residence, size of office space); well-connected; carefully selects and enlists others to buttress his or her swollen sense of importance. If male, he may have a "trophy wife."
- The person is ambitious to the point of being exploitative. She makes the environment resonate to her own needs.
- The person reacts explosively if his "false front" (projected image) is questioned or exposed. Perceived threats can trigger rage.
- The person is competitive, even to the point of finding enemies who aren't there.

Not good

Mother

Yes!

The Circle of Charm

James Masterson notes that narcissistic functioning is actually the outcome of low self-esteem. It is a defense against insecurity and abandonment. Outwardly vain, the narcissist is inwardly impaired. "The narcissist resembles a psychological turtle with a hard, impenetrable shell," Masterson concludes, but it has "an equally soft, fearful center."[5] The narcissist is not as certain as he or she looks, as evidenced by his or her supersensitivity to criticism. The illusion of stability is sustained by appearance. The narcissist is a master at denying reality, projecting an image of invincibility or charisma and coercing the world to refuel his specialness. There is no transparency in narcissistic functioning. It's all varnish and veneer—with lots of charm.

The functioning of the charmer and the charmed is one of mutual reinforcement—and self-deception. Neither one wants to know the truth. A person needs to be special and a group of people feeds the specialness. One radiates glory and others bask in that person's glow. One projects the image of self-confidence and the second party idealizes the person who can be so certain, so self-assured. Each needs the other. Their relationship is one of emotional fusion, for neither is able to stand back and see what is happening. The dynamics of narcissism revolve around the lack of self-knowledge. So one person remains intoxicated with all the praise and adulation he manipulates from others, and the others are enthralled to be associated with someone larger than life.

Those who function narcissistically do well so long as they have people who adore them. But some can be so insecure inside that they must ensure their specialness with more and more admirers. They thrive on the ecstasy of numbers. The narcissist functions like a magnet, possessing the power of attraction. People caught in the spell surrender obediently. Under the spell of enchantment, they become dedicated followers as impervious to reason and truth as infatuated lovers. Many of the disciples of narcissists are vulnerable, lonely, and searching souls who *some church people + volunteers* ↑

mistake the charm, self-confidence, and certainty for substance, when in reality it is pretentious fluff and feathers.

In the circle of charm, there are no checks and balances. Groupthink develops. Not surprisingly, many narcissistic leaders shield their swooning constituency from outside influences. They demonize outsiders who might potentially uncover the truth of things or expose the charismatic figure. In the circle of charm, the lights glare, but they don't reveal.

Those who are most vulnerable to charm are those people or groups who need stimulation outside themselves. Often they are depressed or demoralized. Many are looking for a high, some brightness or good feeling in their lives, to make them special. Masterson calls them "closet narcissists."[6] Instead of investing their own specialness in a grandiose self, they invest in an omnipotent other. By associating with the special person, they get dusted with the same magic and importance.

Narcissistic Supplies

Narcissists are attracted to professions that have ample narcissistic supplies structured into the nature of the work. A graduate student (whose name I don't recall) sent me a copy of his Ph.D. dissertation in which he discussed his finding that the three professions most alluring to people who need specialness are sales, entertainment, and public ministry. Modeling, acting, and politics are additional professions that can allow narcissists to go undetected, because they provide protective environments—that is, they offer continuous feedback, keeping the balloon of self-importance well inflated. The narcissist can thrive for years without realizing that the core of his or her life is empty and that beneath the narcissistic glitter is a false and an impaired self. (Not all people in these professions are narcissistic, but there is a higher proportion relative to other professions.)

Masterson tells the story of 12 individuals who called him for therapy. The calls came immediately after Masterson had been quoted in the *New York Times* about the major symptoms of narcissism. Each of the 12 came to him for an evaluation. Each indeed exhibited the very symptoms Masterson had noted in the newspaper article. All wanted to continue therapy, but Masterson did not have time to see them. He referred them to associates. None returned for treatment. Masterson saw this as just another symptom of their narcissism. They wanted to use Masterson as a narcissistic supply rather than seek help. Because of Masterson's reputation, being in therapy with him would greatly reinforce their special images of themselves, while being in therapy with someone else would not supply them with grandiosity.

Bent on being successful, the narcissist seeks out people who can contribute to that end. The narcissist needs the limelight. Others must play supporting roles. Many narcissists are workaholics who overwork their staffs and demand devotion from office workers. In return, the staff members receive full praise for their work. Many staff, over a period of time, begin to see through the empty praise and the false facade of concern for supporters. They realize that they are valued only insofar as they reinforce the narcissist's own glory. They are mere suppliers. But staff members need to be careful not to expose the sham. The narcissist works hard at eliminating feelings of shame. Shame involves exposure. Any shattering of his projected self-image endangers the reinforcing grandiosity supply. The narcissist will lash out in rage against the whistleblower.

Avoiding the Circle

When people are emotionally interlocked through charm, grandiosity, and need, they have insufficient distance to see what is really happening. In many situations, congregations prefer the glow of the moment to making decisions that dull the glow but put the congregation in a better light for the future.

Charisma is in the eyes of the beholder. To idealize someone as infinitely wise, incredibly kind, or unbelievably powerful can make a person feel safe. The admirer becomes childlike, diminishing his own self in order to gain from the magnification of the charmer, and suspends judgment. The narcissist and the narcissistic supplier form a system out of two impaired selves.

The need to appear larger than life and the need to believe in the superspecialness of others may provide solace and comfort in a threatening world. But it also limits authenticity, awareness, and intimacy. Impaired selves create a false reality. When the circle of charm fails, charisma may be seen for what it is—a cheap substitute for *charis,* the biblical word for grace.

Charisma gives the appearance of being able to heal and save, but it cannot deliver the goods. It is a charm that seeks to use, not free, us. By virtue of their specialness, narcissistic people believe they are entitled to control and manipulate other people. They use other people's devotion toward them as sustenance for their own need for specialness—a way to redeem their impaired selves.

In the circle of charm, there is no freedom. Two shaky selves are foolishly and slavishly connected. Even more, the people of the charm bring incredible damage to a congregation. The charmer is often involved in sexual misconduct, misuse of funds, or in setting oppositional groups. The charmed can be so blinded by the charmer that they defend the narcissistic behavior, even encourage it. They cannot face the truth of the damage wrought by the spellbinder.

Congregations

Congregations can be warehouses of narcissistic supplies. Congregations that idealize the office of ministry and those who fill it still exist, as do clergy who greatly need a daily replenishment of approval and specialness. When each feeds the other for years, allowing charm to glue them together, neither side will easily let the other go.

Other congregations attract narcissistic clergy because they need someone outside of themselves to motivate them. They seek a savior figure. Looking for this type of leader (who is frequently referred to as strong, dynamic, or a champion), members don't realize that they set themselves up to be the prey of narcissists. Members see the charm, certainty, and coolness and go into a trance, believing they have found the real thing.

Sometimes the person who needs mirroring of her greatness is a layperson in a position of power or influence. If charming and quite pious, this person can hold the congregation in her narcissistic grip for a long time. She is extraordinarily special, therefore given homage and honor by many members.

Congregations like Holy Church are magnets for charismatic leaders. Holy Church has grown phenomenally. Its rapid growth has been the envy of other congregations. Pastor Ken has served them for five years and has spearheaded much of their growth. He has a knack for conversing with others. He has a winsome, outgoing, and witty sense about him. About one third of those who have joined Holy Church are there because of Rev. Ken's personal contact with them. Many of them have not belonged to a church since their youth or have not attended regularly before.

Nonetheless, all that glittered was not gold. People had begun to notice that lay leaders were leaving their positions before their term expired. Still, the resignations had been attributed to the lay people's overwork or other commitments. When five of the twelve governing board members had left within two months of each other, a group in the church had wondered why. Pastor Ken had said they left for various reasons, as if the resignations were all coincidental. Several months later, however, it became public that two had resigned because Pastor Ken threatened them when they had questioned his authority. A third had revealed to close friends that Pastor Ken had made an overt sexual advance. A fourth had said that Pastor Ken was a "great pastor, but a tyrant." The fifth had mentioned Ken's total revision of her committee's work.

When a consultant had come to the congregation eight months later, he had discovered Ken's pattern of lies, questionable use of financial funds, and instances of rage. A good number of members had rejected the consultant's findings. Rev. Ken, they said, had to be a strong leader; after all, look at the results of their growth. They simply would not listen to anything that put Ken in a negative light. Ken, meanwhile, had kept them in the charmed position by noting their courage, greater commitment, or intelligence. One of his favorite comments spoken privately to people who had questioned him was: "I can't believe you're so naive as to accept that."

He would not accept responsibility for any of the items the consultant discovered, dismissing the consultant as inexperienced. For five years Ken had led the congregation to believe that the judicatory had incompetents on its staff. He thereby shielded members from a second source of objectivity. But the tension had intensified. About 12 months later, Ken resigned suddenly, blaming the "sick, wounded" people for his undoing. Many in his adoration club joined him in exiting. They had psychically clumped together—the people of the charm.

Avoiding the Circle

What can a congregation do to detect a potential problem? When is the circle of charm most likely to form?

An individual or group can ask a set of questions about the pastor or lay leader and another set of questions concerning themselves.

Questions about a Pastor or Lay Leader

- Is this person too good to be true? Do we sense that something isn't right or missing when we talk to the person or observe his or her behavior?

- Have we carefully reviewed the person's history, what preceded this moment, what happened elsewhere?
- Why doesn't this person show any weaknesses or vulnerabilities? Why does this person always seem to be on top of the world? Did this person have disciples, groupies, or blind followers in past work situations?
- Does the person blame others, take the role of victim, or claim complete innocence of any past trouble?

Questions for Ourselves

- Does our congregation have a good set of checks and balances? Can someone tilt the balance favorably in his or her direction without much effort? Is our congregation looking for a gem, a superstar, a mighty motivator, and does our congregation think it is special?
- Do we use superlative words to describe what we want in a pastor or leader—dynamic, sharp, terrific, passionate, charismatic?
- Are we looking for a savior? Do we have lots of resources? Is there great potential for growth?
- Is there an adequate feedback system? Can someone control information? Can people be propagandized?

Narcissism is a disease of relationship, a disease that springs from a failure to make meaningful relationship to oneself and others. Its opposite is an attitude towards life that stresses the importance of commitment, involvement, love, sacrifice.[7]
—Danah Zohar

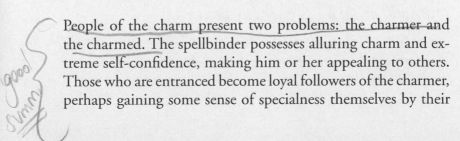

People of the charm present two problems: the charmer and the charmed. The spellbinder possesses alluring charm and extreme self-confidence, making him or her appealing to others. Those who are entranced become loyal followers of the charmer, perhaps gaining some sense of specialness themselves by their strong attachment to the charismatic person. I once heard someone refer to this situation as "*gilt* by association." In their emotional trance, the charmed fail to see what they fail to see. So neither the charmer nor the charmed is capable of much self-awareness. Nonetheless, the charmer brings havoc to relationships. Others who know and see it are ineffective in dealing with the "charmer/charmed" problem if they think being nice or expressing goodwill will change things. The game is domination for the narcissist, not cooperation. A person functioning in a narcissistic way must be held accountable for his behaviors.

Notes

Preface

1. Murray Bowen was the director of the Georgetown Family Center in Washington, D.C., now known as the Bowen Center for the Study of the Family. In 1980 Bowen made a distinction between his theory and those of others in the family systems movement. Bowen Theory is known for its unique concepts, such as the "emotional process," "differentiation" and "the togetherness forces." To distinguish his ideas from others in the family systems movement, Bowen simply referred to them as "Bowen Theory."

2. Peter L. Steinke, *Healthy Congregations: A Systems Approach* (Herndon, VA: Alban Institute, 2007), xi.

Chapter 1, Anxious Souls

1. Michael E. Kerr and Murray Bowen, *Family Evaluation: An Approach Based on Bowen Theory* (New York: W. W. Norton, 1988), 112.

2. Richard Restak, *Poe's Heart and the Mountain Climber: Exploring the Effect of Anxiety on Our Brains and Our Culture* (New York: Harmony Books, 2004), 10.

3. Presented by Edwin H. Friedman in a workshop, "Post Graduate Seminar In Family Emotional Process," Bethesda, Maryland, 1990.

4. John Updike, *Collected Poems: 1953–1993* (New York: Alfred A Knopf, 1995), 28.

5.   Dean R. Hoge and Jacqueline E. Wenger, *Pastors in Transition: Why Clergy Leave Local Church Ministry* (Grand Rapids, MI: Wm. B. Eerdmans, 2005), 76–79.

Chapter 2, The Balancing Act

1.   Danah Zohar and Ian Marshall, *The Quantum Society: Mind, Physics, and a New Social Vision* (New York: William Morrow, 1994), 23–25.

2.   Norman Cousins, *Medicine as a Human Experience,* ed. D. E. Reiser, and D. H. Rosen (Baltimore, MD: University Park Press, 1984), xvi.

3.   David Bohm quoted in Graham Alexander and Ben Renshaw, *SuperCoaching: The Missing Ingredient for High Performance* (New York: Random House Business Books, 2005), 42.

4.   Margaret J. Wheatley, *Leadership and the New Science: Learning about Organization from an Orderly Universe* (San Francisco: Berrett-Koehler Publishers, 1992), 24. See also Zohar and Marshall, *The Quantum Society,* 62-63, and John Briggs and F. David Peat, *Turbulent Mirror* (New York: Harper and Row, 1989), 153–158.

5.   Frank Vertosick Jr., *The Genius Within: Discovering the Intelligence of Every Living Thing* (New York: Harcourt, 2002), 180–185.

6.   Larry L. Rasmussen, *Earth Community and Earth Ethics* (Maryknoll, NY: Orbis Books, 1997), 29.

7.   Murray Bowen, *Family Theory in Clinical Practice* (Northvale, NJ: Jason Aronson, 1978, 1985), 496.

8.   Parker J. Palmer, *The Courage to Teach* (San Francisco: John Wiley, 1998), 72.

9.   Rainer Maria Rilke, *Letters to a Young Poet* (New York: Vintage Books, 1984), 74.

10.   Ibid., 69.

11.   Bowen, 277.

12.   James Surowiecki, *The Wisdom of Crowds: Why the Many Are Smarter Than the Few and How Collective Wisdom Shapes Business, Economics, Societies, and Nations* (New York: Doubleday, 2004), 42.

13.   Bowen, 485.

Chapter 3, The Nonanxious Presence

1. Harriet Lerner, *Fear and Other Uninvited Guests* (New York: HarperCollins, 2004), 59.

2. Robert Ornstein and David Sobel, *The Healing Brain* (New York: Simon and Schuster, 1987), 246–247.

3. Daniel N. T. Perkins, *Leading at the Edge* (New York: American Management Association, 2000), 30.

4. Ibid., 25.

5. Ibid., 44.

6. John Gottman, *Why Marriages Succeed or Fail: And How You Can Make Yours Last* (New York: Simon and Schuster, 1994), 39–43, 66–67, 97–98.

Chapter 4, Holy Tissue

1. Shelley E. Taylor, *The Tending Instinct: How Nurturing Is Essential to Who We Are and How We Live* (New York: Times Books, 2002), 20–22.

2. Elkhonon Goldberg, *The Executive Brain: Frontal Lobes And the Civilized Mind* (New York: Oxford University Press, 2001), 2, 23.

3. Malcolm MacMillan, *An Odd Kind of Fame: Stories of Phineas Gage* (Cambridge, MA: The MIT Press, 2000), 93.

4. William Shakespeare, *The Life and Death of King John,* act 5, scene 7, line 5, The Oxford Shakespeare, ed. W. J. Craig (London: Oxford University Press, 1914), at http://www.bartleby.com/70/2557. html (accessed Sept. 12, 2006).

5. Candace Pert quoted in Judith Hooper and Dick Teresi, *The 3-Pound Universe: Revolutionary Discoveries about the Brain—From the Chemistry of the Mind to the New Frontiers of the Soul* (New York: Putnam Books, 1986), 42.

6. Ibid., 390.

7. Joseph Chilton Pearce, *The Biology of Transcendence: A Blueprint of the Human Spirit* (Rochester, VT: Park Street Press, 2002), 41.

8. Lerner, 2–3.

Chapter 5, Influencing the Emotional Field

1.   Daniel Goleman, Richard Bayatzis, and Annie McKae, *Primal Leadership: Realize the Power of Emotional Intelligence* (Boston: Harvard Business School Press, 2002), 172.

2.   Presented by Edwin H. Friedman in the workshop "Post-Graduate Seminar in Family Emotional Process," Bethesda, MD, 1994.

3.   Edwin H. Friedman, *A Failure of Nerve: Leadership in the Age of the Quick Fix* (Bethesda, MD: Friedman Estate, 1999), 12.

4.   Ibid., 180, 187.

5.   Ibid., 170.

6.   Diane Ackerman, *An Alchemy of Mind: The Marvel and Mystery of the Brain* (New York: Scribner, 2004), 175.

7.   Nancy Tatom Ammerman, *Congregation and Community* (New Brunswick, NJ: Rutgers University Press, 1997), 345.

Chapter 6, The Essential Edge

1.   Roland Barthes, *Sade/Fourier/Loyola,* trans. Richard Miller (New York: Hill and Wang, 1976), 52–53.

2.   Theodore Schwenk, *Sensitive Chaos* (New York: Rudolf Steiner Press, 1965), 58.

3.   Sherwin B. Nuland, *The Wisdom of the Body* (New York: Alfred A. Knopf, 1997), 207.

4.   Ibid., 210.

5.   Lewis Thomas, *The Medusa and the Snail: More Notes of a Biology Watcher* (New York: Bantam Books, 1979), 91.

6.   Paul Brand, *Fearfully and Wonderfully Made* (Grand Rapids, MI: Zondervan Books, 1987), 29.

7.   Thomas, 76.

8.   Ibid., 145.

9.   Information on immune response based on a *New York Times* article. Also see "toll-like receptors" on the Wikipedia Web site at http://en.wikipedia.org/wiki/Toll_like_receptors (accessed Sept. 13, 2006).

10. Information about cancer cells from conversations in June 2006 with Dr. Steve Houston, a cancer specialist in Austin, TX.

11. Larry Rasmussen, "Shaping Communities," *Practicing Our Faith: A Way of Life for a Searching People,* ed. Dorothy C. Bass (San Francisco: Jossey-Bass, 1997), 120.

Chapter 7, We versus They

1. Adam Gopnik, "Read All About It," *New Yorker,* Dec. 12, 1984, 84–102.

2. Garret Keizer, *The Enigma of Anger: Essays on a Sometimes Deadly Sin* (San Francisco, CA: Jossey-Bass, 2002), 292.

3. Hugh Halverstadt, *Managing Church Conflict* (Louisville, KY: Westminster/John Knox Press, 1991), 2.

4. Edwin Friedman, *Generation to Generation* (New York: Guilford Press, 1985), 232.

5. Keizer, 88.

6. Edward de Bono, *Conflicts: A Better Way to Resolve Them* (New York: Penguin Books, 1985), 25.

7. Ibid., 76.

8. Peter Senge et al, *The Fifth Discipline Fieldbook* (New York: Doubleday, 1994), 197.

9. Evert Van de Vliert, *Complex Interpersonal Conflict Behavior: Theoretical Frontiers* (East Sussex, UK: Psychology Press, 1997), 142.

Chapter 8, Rocking the Emotional Boat

1. Walter Brueggeman, *The Covenanted Self: Exploration in Law and Covenant* (Minneapolis: Fortress Press, 1998), 16.

2. Ronald Heifetz and Donald Laurie, "The Work of Leadership," *Harvard Business Review,* December 2001, 131.

3. Ronald A. Heifetz and Martin Linsky, *Leadership on the Line: Staying Alive through the Dangers of Leading* (Boston: Harvard Business School Press, 2002), 18–48.

4.   Sherwin B. Nuland, *The Doctor's Plague: Germs, Childhood, Fever and the Strange Story of Ignac Semmelweiss* (New York: W. W. Norton, 2003). This brief narrative is derived from Nuland's observations.

5.   Heifetz and Linsky, 30.

6.   Leo Tolstoy quoted in James Gleick, *Chaos: Making a New Science* (New York: Penguin Books, 1987), 38.

7.   Elkhonon Goldberg, *The Wisdom Paradox: How Your Mind Can Grow Stronger as Your Brain Grows Older* (New York: Gotham Books, 2005), 211.

8.   Rollo May, *The Courage to Create* (New York: W. W. Norton, 1975), 120–122.

Chapter 9, To Challenge or to Survive

1.   Michael E. Kerr and Murray Bowen, *Family Evaluation: An Approach Based on Bowen Theory* (New York: W. W. Norton, 1988), 103–105.

2.   Elie Wiesel, *Wise Men and Their Tales: Portraits of Biblical, Talmudic, and Hasidic Masters* (New York: Schocken Books, 2003), 43.

3.   Ibid.

4.   Edwin H. Friedman, *A Failure of Nerve: Leadership in the Age of the Quick Fix* (Bethesda, MD: Friedman Estate, 1999), 35.

5.   Based on an English translation taken from http://www.brainyquote.com/quotes/quotes/a/aristotle132211.html.

6.   Henri J. M. Nouwen, *The Dance of Life: Weaving Sorrows and Blessing into One Joyful Step,* ed. Michael Ford (Notre Dame, IN: Ava Maria Press, 2005), 156.

7.   Ibid.

Postscript, People of the Charm

1.   This essay has been adapted from an article in my newsletter *New Creation,* Vol. 2, No. 1, Winter 2000.

2.   Alexander Lowen, *Narcissism: Denial of the True Self* (New York: Macmillan, 1983), 26–27.

3.   James F. Masterson, *The Search for the Real Self: Unmasking the Personality Disorder of Our Age* (New York: Free Press, 1988), 91.

4.   Lowen, 25.

5.   Masterson, 174.

6.   Ibid., 103.

7.   Danah Zohar, *The Quantum Self: Human Nature and Consciousness Defined by the New Physics* (New York: William Morrow, 1990), 155.